TIME

2007
The Year in Review

By the Editors of TIME

TIME

MANAGING EDITOR Richard Stengel
DEPUTY MANAGING EDITORS Priscilla Painton, Adi Ignatius,
Michael Elliott

2007: The Year in Review

EDITOR Kelly Knauer
DESIGNER Ellen Fanning
PICTURE EDITOR Patricia Cadley
WRITER/RESEARCH DIRECTOR Matthew McCann Fenton
COPY EDITOR Bruce Christopher Carr

TIME INC. HOME ENTERTAINMENT
PUBLISHER Richard Fraiman
GENERAL MANAGER Steven Sandonato
EXECUTIVE DIRECTOR, MARKETING SERVICES Carol Pittard
DIRECTOR, RETAIL & SPECIAL SALES Tom Mifsud
DIRECTOR, NEW PRODUCT DEVELOPMENT Peter Harper
ASSISTANT DIRECTOR, BRAND MARKETING Laura Adam
ASSOCIATE COUNSEL Helen Wan
BOOK PRODUCTION MANAGER Jonathan Polsky
DESIGN AND PREPRESS MANAGER Anne-Michelle Gallero
SENIOR BRAND MANAGER Joy Butts
ASSOCIATE BRAND MANAGER Shelley Rescober

SPECIAL THANKS
Bozena Bannett, Glenn Buonocore, Suzanne Janso, Robert Marasco, Brooke Reger,
Mary Sarro-Waite, Ilene Schreider, Adriana Tierno, Alex Voznesenskiy

ISBN 10: 1-933821-22-1
ISBN 13: 978-1-933821-22-1
ISBN 1097-5721

We welcome your comments and suggestions about Time Books. Please write to us at:
Time Books • Attention: Book Editors • PO Box 11016 • Des Moines, IA 50336-1016

If you would like to order any of our hardcover Collector's Edition books,
please call us at 1-800-327-6388 (Monday through Friday, 7 a.m.–8 p.m.,
or Saturday, 7 a.m.–6 p.m., Central time).

PRINTED IN THE UNITED STATES OF AMERICA

Front cover photography credits, clockwise from top left: Petraeus: Brooks Kraft—Corbis;
Pelosi: Jason Reed—Reuters/Landov; firefighters: K.C. Alfred—SDU-T—ZUMA Press;
Virginia Tech: Win McNamee —Getty Images; monks: AFP/Getty Images; Bonds: Rich
Pilling—MLB Photos/Getty Images; bridge: Heather Munro—Polaris; Williams:
Adrian Dennis—Getty Images; Schwarzenegger: Ben Baker—Redux; Johnson: Frank
Wolfe—LBJ Library/AP Images

Back cover photography credits, clockwise from top left: Woods: Stuart Franklin—Getty
Images; flood: Daniel Berehulak—Getty Images; Jobs: Joe Pugliese—Corbis Outline;
Branson: Brian Smith—Corbis Outline; laser: Yuri Beletsky—ESO

KRISTA KENNELL—ZUMA PRESS

California burning *The Golden State was hammered by wildfires in the spring of 2007, but they paled in comparison to the immense blazes that ripped across Southern California in late October. At left, a helicopter pumps water to fight the fires from a golf course pond in the Stevenson Ranch development in Santa Clarita, north of Los Angeles, on Oct. 22. In a single day the flames from the blaze, dubbed the Magic Fire, charred more than 1,000 acres in this area*

CONTENTS

Kickin' back *Oregon gas-station owner Kent Couch, 48, enjoys his view of the Cascade Mountains from a lawn chair that is airborne thanks to 105 helium balloons, on July 7, 2007. Flight plan for the 193-mile journey: ascend by releasing water used for ballast; follow prevailing winds; descend by shooting balloons with a BB-gun*

Baquba, Iraq, March 15

Iraq the Eternal

Silent and immobile, aged and inscrutable, commanding the focus of the picture yet unapproachable—everything about the Iraqi woman in this photograph seems indicative of the deep cultural divisions that continue to thwart Americans' attempts to understand the land they invaded in 2003, much less bring order and security to it.

Four years into Operation Iraqi Freedom, the U.S. mission in Iraq continued to dominate the news, with the Bush Administration adopting a "surge" strategy that sent an additional 30,000 soldiers to the nation, beginning in February. By June, the number of U.S. troops in Iraq reached a new high of 168,000, even as a bevy of opinion polls recorded the increasing dissatisfaction of the American public with President George W. Bush's conduct of the war.

In this picture, U.S. troops who have just nabbed a militant as he was putting an improvised bomb beside the road have detained other local men suspected of being accomplices or sympathizers.

YURI KOZYREV FOR TIME

"Godzilla Winds"

The Santa Ana winds, which form in the high deserts of California and Nevada and blow west to the Pacific, have often been midwives to disaster in Southern California. But in 2007 they struck with epic force. Beginning overnight on Oct. 20, unusually fierce winds stoked fires that burst into life throughout a landscape parched in the past year by the worst drought in Los Angeles' recorded history. By midweek, at least 20 separate blazes formed pockets of fire running from the Mexican border north to Simi Valley, outside Los Angeles. Some 7,000 firefighters were recruited from around the country to battle the flames. At right, firefighter Sean Threlfall works to secure a home in Poway, in hard-hit San Diego County.

By Oct. 25, the flames had consumed more than 400,000 acres, destroyed more than 2,000 houses and forced the temporary evacuation of as many as 1 million people—the biggest mass migration in the U.S. since Hurricane Katrina. "These were Godzilla winds," NASA-JPL climatologist Bill Patzert told TIME. More bad news: the Santa Anas usually don't peak until the winter.

K.C. ALFRED—SAN DIEGO UNION TRIBUNE—ZUMA PRESS

Poway, Calif., Oct. 22

Virginia Tech, Blacksburg, Va., April 16

IMAGES

Horror on Campus

"I'm going to kill people at VTech today," student Cho Seung-Hui, 23, wrote in an online forum early on the morning of April 16. A bit before, he made a videotape in which he ranted into the camera about his desire to get even with "rich brats" who had trust funds and gold necklaces and Mercedes. "You have never felt a single ounce of pain in your whole lives," he declared.

Hours later, around 9 a.m., freshman Michael Cunningham was sleeping in his dorm, West Ambler Johnston Hall, when he heard sounds like three doors slamming. "It was so windy on Monday, and many students leave their windows open at night," he said. "So we assumed that it was doors being shut by a wind gust." He went back to sleep. Those sounds appear to have been the shots that killed freshman Emily Hilscher

("Pixie" on her MySpace page), 19, and her next-door neighbor, residential adviser Ryan Clark, 22.

Cho took a break from his murdering spree to send his video rant to NBC News in New York City via express mail, then returned to the campus around 11 a.m. and shot 30 more people to death, before taking his own life. University officials, suspecting they were dealing with a killer seeking revenge in a personal drama rather than a psychopath, had failed to lock down the campus—or even inform students about the two early-morning murders.

Above, police carry victims out of Norris Hall, scene of Cho's most deadly rampage. In the days afterward, a litany of overlooked warning signs would emerge, indicating that Cho should have been recognized as dangerous. But as one of the killer's classmates tearfully said later, "I kept having to tell myself there is no way we could have known this was coming."

Ramadi, Anbar province, Iraq, Jan. 17

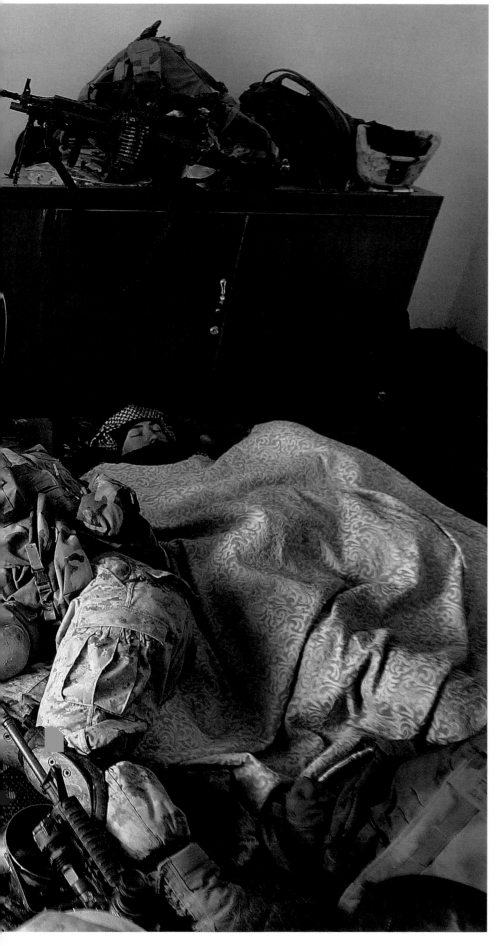

Ramadi Reveille

Moving stealthily on a thankless mission, a U.S. Marine awakens a comrade to take his turn on guard duty during the first stages of a U.S. operation to secure the city of Ramadi in the Anbar province of Iraq. The Marines, working in tandem with Iraqi army troops, swept into the area on Jan. 17 in a major surprise offensive intended to curb insurgent activity in Ramadi, at the time an area where U.S. casualty rates were among the highest in the nation. The Americans are sleeping in the home of a man identified as a former financier of local insurgents.

In a welcome about-face, Sunni leaders in Anbar province began working with the U.S. troops to bring order to the area, at the expense of their ancient enemies, the minority Shi'ite residents. By September, the Bush Administration was hailing peaceful Ramadi as a success story, and President George W. Bush paid a surprise visit to the area on Sept. 3. Ten days later, the Sunni sheik who had become a key ally of the U.S., Abdul Sattar Buzaigh al-Rishawi, was killed by a roadside bomb.

Minneapolis, Aug. 1

A Bridge Too Frail

Dennis and Jamie Winegar of Houston were admiring the view of the Mississippi River as they drove across Minneapolis' Interstate 35W during the evening rush hour on Aug. 1, when the roadway began to shake beneath them. "I slammed on my brakes and saw something in front of me disappear," Dennis recalled, "and then my car pointed straight down, and we fell." After dropping more than 50 ft., the Winegars' car landed among others on the collapsed roadbed. "When I got out, there was a car lodged underneath me and one right next to me," said Dennis Winegar.

Jamie Winegar remembers dazed survivors assisting one another off the bridge, while she was aided by people who had witnessed the disaster and launched an impromptu rescue operation within minutes. "There were a bunch of people right around there helping everyone," she says. "Angels is what I call them." But the angels couldn't help all the victims: 13 people died in the tragedy, and hundreds more were injured. A new bridge will open by the end of 2008.

Home, Home On the Range

Plagued by a genocidal civil war in its Darfur region, Sudan has become a byword for bad news. So it was all the more stunning when wildlife conservationists reported some very good tidings from South Sudan, scene of a separate, long-running civil war that was resolved in 2005 with a cease-fire and the creation of a separate Government of Southern Sudan. The peace pact allowed scientists from the U.S.-based Wildlife Conservation Society to conduct the first aerial wildlife survey of the area since 1983.

Scientists feared the worst: similar conflicts had threatened entire species in such nations as Angola, Mozambique and the Central African Republic. But in June, the exuberant trackers announced they had found enormous herds of migrating species that had survived the war, including 1.2 million white-eared kob and Topi antelope, at right, and Mongalla gazelles, some parading in processions up to 50 miles long. The government vowed to protect the beasts, whose numbers may rival or even surpass those of the famed Serengeti herds to the south, in hopes of creating an ecotourism industry in the long-suffering nation.

PAUL ELKIN & J. MICHAEL FAY

Southern Sudan, January 2007

Rangoon (Yangon), Sept. 26

"Democracy!"

"They pour south from the Shwedagon, the immense golden pagoda that is Burma's most revered Buddhist monument, in an unbroken, mile-long column —barefoot, chanting, clutching pictures of Buddha … a solid stream of red and orange, like blood vessels giving life to an oxygen-starved body." Thus an eye-witness, Scottish writer Andrew Marshall, described the massive street protests that roused Burma (Myanmar) in September on TIME.COM. The monks were joined by tens of thousands of civilians, shouting "Democracy!" Burma has been ruled by a harshly repressive military junta since 1962, and as a result, said Marshall, "people grew poorer, stalked by disease and malnutrition. Inflation lurched ever upward. Schools and hospitals crumbled with neglect."

On Sept. 26 the junta struck back, shutting off Burma's access to the outside world, including Internet service. Riot police and soldiers moved against the monks and other protesters in a brutal crackdown. The number of those who died may have exceeded 1,000; the total may never be known.

Bania Shanta, Bangladesh, Nov. 17

Swept Away

Bangladeshis are steeped in catastrophe: their nation is perched at the northern end of the Bay of Bengal, where giant tropical storms are funneled between land masses, gaining strength before making landfall in one of the world's poorest and most densely populated countries. In 1991 Cyclone Gorky killed at least 138,000 people, and 1970's Bhola claimed as many as 500,000 lives. The 2007 monsoon rains in Bangladesh were the heaviest in seven years. They bred mudslides as well as floods, killing 119 residents of seaport city Chittagong. At the monsoon season's peak, around Aug. 1, some 5 million Bangladeshis were left homeless.

Yet the monsoons turned out to be only a warm-up. On Nov. 15-16, Cyclone Sidr, a Category 4 storm, swept through the nation, flattening houses, damaging roads and destroying thousands of acres of crops. More than 3,000 people were killed, far fewer than in earlier disasters. But that must have offered little consolation to the woman at left, whom neighbors identified as Supna. The storm took her house, her livelihood and her husband; friends said she had not spoken a word since it passed.

PHOTOGRAPH BY SAIFUL HUQ OMI—POLARIS

Abandon Ship!

Almost 100 years ago, the world was riveted by tales of Antarctic exploration, and particularly by the famed "Race to the Pole," in which Briton Robert Falcon Scott and Norwegian Roald Amundsen each claimed to have been the first to reach the South Pole.

In 1969 modern-day adventurer Lars-Eric Linblad put the excitement of a journey to the Antarctic within the reach of anyone who could afford it, when he launched the first passenger ship designed expressly for polar voyages, M.S. *Explorer.*

After decades of service, *Explorer* sank on Nov. 23, apparently after a collision with ice put a gash in its specially reinforced hull. The precise cause of the sinking was unclear at press time. All 154 people aboard were rescued after spending several hours in lifeboats; no panic was reported. These pictures—whose quality is poor, given the conditions under which they were shot—show the foundering ship; the rope ladders used by passengers and crew to evacuate the vessel; the orange life rafts, enclosed to counter extreme weather in the polar regions; and the safe arrival of the rescued passengers at Fildes Bay on King George Island.

PHOTOGRAPHS BY CHILEAN AIR FORCE—AP IMAGES (4)

Bansfield Bay and King George Island, Great Southern Ocean, Nov. 23

Arlington National Cemetery, Arlington, Va., May 27

Memorial Day

Mary McHugh, 26, mourns her fiancé, U.S. Army Sergeant James Regan, on the Sunday of Memorial Day weekend. Regan, also 26, was killed Feb. 9, 2007, by an improvised explosive device that detonated near his vehicle while he was on patrol outside Baghdad. Regan, a member of the 3rd Battalion's 75th Ranger Regiment, was a native of Manhasset, N.Y., and a star lacrosse player in high school and at Duke University. "When I heard the news, I felt like I was getting hit by a truck," his high school lacrosse coach, Jack Moran, told Long Island's *Newsday* newspaper. "You couldn't ask for a better person." Regan had received a scholarship to attend law school after graduating from Duke but chose to become an Army Ranger. "He said, 'If I don't do it, then who will do it?'" McHugh told *Newsday*.

On his blog, photographer John Moore wrote, "Some people felt the photo ... was too intimate, too personal. Like many who have seen the picture, I felt overwhelmed by her grief, and moved by the love she felt for her fallen sweetheart."

As of Sept. 18, 2007, 3,791 U.S. military personnel had died in Iraq and 27,936 had been wounded.

Charting 2007

A different way to look at the year—as TIME designers see it

■ Obesity in America

Americans keep packing on the pounds, according to the fourth annual obesity report from the Trust for America's Health. In the previous year, the 2007 study found, obesity rates had gone up in 31 states, and no states had shrinking rates. The report found that two-thirds of U.S. adults are overweight or obese, 60% of the population in 32 states is overweight or obese and more than 30% of all Mississippians are obese—the highest percentage recorded for any state ever. Outdoorsy Colorado is still the least overweight state.

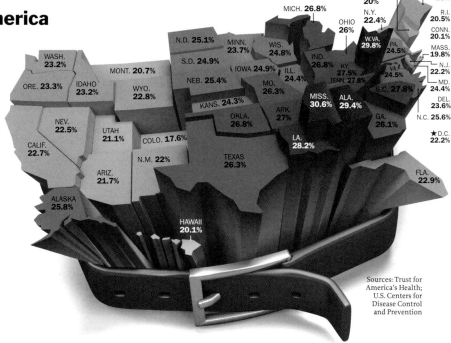

N.H. **22.4%**
VT. **20%**
MICH. **26.8%**
ME. **23%**
N.Y. **22.4%**
OHIO **26%**
R.I. **20.5%**
CONN. **20.1%**
W.VA. **29.8%**
PA. **24.5%**
MASS. **19.8%**
N.J. **22.2%**
MD. **24.4%**
VA. **24.5%**
DEL. **23.6%**
N.C. **25.6%**
★ D.C. **22.2%**
N.D. **25.1%**
MINN. **23.7%**
WIS. **24.8%**
WASH. **23.2%**
S.D. **24.9%**
IND. **26.8%**
KY. **27.5%**
TENN. **27.8%**
S.C. **27.8%**
MONT. **20.7%**
IOWA **24.9%**
ILL. **24.4%**
ORE. **23.3%**
IDAHO **23.2%**
WYO. **22.8%**
NEB. **25.4%**
MO. **26.3%**
MISS. **30.6%**
ALA. **29.4%**
GA. **26.1%**
NEV. **22.5%**
UTAH **21.1%**
COLO. **17.6%**
KANS. **24.3%**
ARK. **27%**
CALIF. **22.7%**
OKLA. **26.8%**
LA. **28.2%**
ARIZ. **21.7%**
N.M. **22%**
TEXAS **26.3%**
FLA. **22.9%**
ALASKA **25.8%**
HAWAII **20.1%**

Sources: Trust for America's Health; U.S. Centers for Disease Control and Prevention

■ Education Report Card

The Department of Education reported that 48 states and the District of Columbia either improved academically or held steady in all categories since the most recent set of national tests in 2005. (Only Rhode Island and North Dakota missed the mark.) Reading scores among fourth-grade students edged up a few points to reach a historic high, as did math scores for both fourth- and eighth-graders. But there wasn't much narrowing of achievement gaps between white and minority students. And there are still far too many kids scoring below basic levels in math and reading.

Percent of students with achievement level below basic

7% to 13%
14% to 16%
17% to 20%
21% to 22%
23% to 26%
27% to 30%
31% to 35%
36% to 52%
53% to 66%

Source: U.S. Department of Education

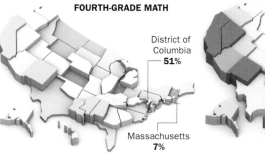

FOURTH-GRADE MATH

District of Columbia **51%**

Massachusetts **7%**

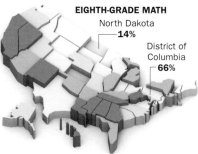

EIGHTH-GRADE MATH

North Dakota **14%**

District of Columbia **66%**

FOURTH-GRADE READING

District of Columbia **61%**

Massachusetts **19%**

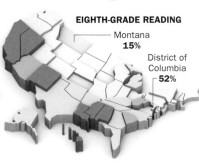

EIGHTH-GRADE READING

Montana **15%**

District of Columbia **52%**

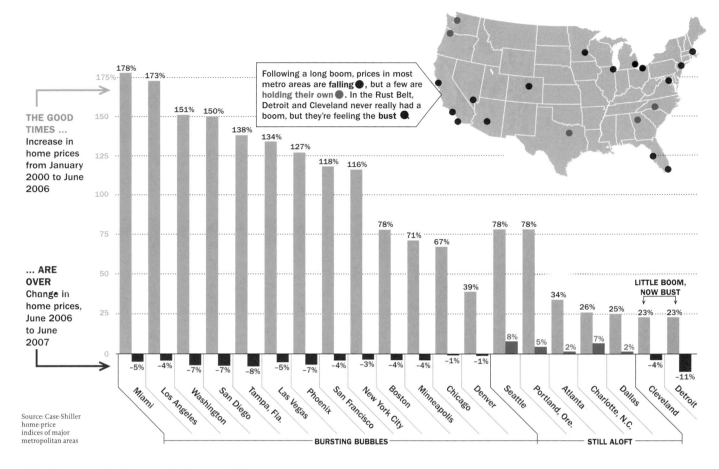

THE GOOD TIMES …
Increase in home prices from January 2000 to June 2006

Following a long boom, prices in most metro areas are **falling** ●, but a few are **holding their own** ●. In the Rust Belt, Detroit and Cleveland never really had a boom, but they're feeling the **bust** ●.

… ARE OVER
Change in home prices, June 2006 to June 2007

City	Boom	Bust
Miami	178%	−5%
Los Angeles	173%	−4%
Washington	151%	−7%
San Diego	150%	−7%
Tampa, Fla.	138%	−8%
Las Vegas	134%	−5%
Phoenix	127%	−7%
San Francisco	118%	−4%
New York City	116%	−3%
Boston	78%	−4%
Minneapolis	71%	−4%
Chicago	67%	−1%
Denver	39%	−1%
Seattle	78%	8%
Portland, Ore.	78%	5%
Atlanta	34%	2%
Charlotte, N.C.	26%	7%
Dallas	25%	2%
Cleveland	23%	−4%
Detroit	23%	−11%

LITTLE BOOM, NOW BUST

BURSTING BUBBLES — STILL ALOFT

Source: Case-Shiller home-price indices of major metropolitan areas

■ Home Prices Take a Dive

After a long, heady ride, home prices began dropping all over America in 2007, and in some places the fall was steep: the price of an average home declined by 11% in Detroit in one year. Yale University economist Robert Shiller has carefully documented America's post-millennium real estate boom and has been warning for years about the inevitable bust. Shiller cobbled together an inflation-adjusted index of home prices going back to 1890, which showed that a) the price runup from 1997 to 2006 was by far the biggest on record, and b) home prices can fall for decades. Ouch! One consolation: that condo you've been eying in Miami Beach may become a good deal cheaper.

ALCOHOL-RELATED TRAFFIC FATALITIES
Percentage of traffic deaths involving at least one vehicle operator with a blood-alcohol content of .08% or more

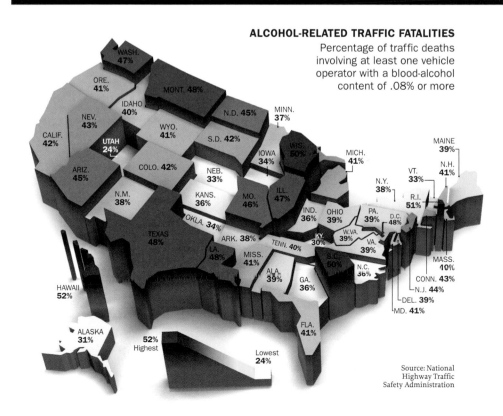

WASH. 47%
ORE. 41%
MONT. 48%
IDAHO 40%
N.D. 45%
MINN. 37%
NEV. 43%
WYO. 41%
S.D. 42%
CALIF. 42%
UTAH 24%
COLO. 42%
IOWA 34%
WIS. 50%
MICH. 41%
MAINE 39%
ARIZ. 45%
NEB. 33%
VT. 33%
N.H. 41%
N.M. 38%
KANS. 36%
MO. 46%
ILL. 47%
IND. 36%
OHIO 39%
N.Y. 38%
R.I. 51%
OKLA. 34%
PA. 39%
D.C. 48%
TEXAS 48%
ARK. 38%
KY. 30%
W.VA. 39%
VA. 39%
MASS. 40%
LA. 48%
TENN. 40%
MISS. 41%
S.C. 50%
N.C. 36%
CONN. 43%
ALA. 39%
GA. 36%
N.J. 44%
DEL. 39%
MD. 41%
HAWAII 52%
FLA. 41%
ALASKA 31%
52% Highest
Lowest 24%

Source: National Highway Traffic Safety Administration

■ State of Drunken Driving

More than 17,600 people were killed in alcohol-related traffic crashes in 2006, according to a 2007 study from the U.S. National Highway Traffic Safety Administration. Utah, whose Mormon population largely shuns drinking, is the state with the lowest rate of alcohol-related fatalities; just 24%. Hawaii has the highest rate: 52% of its fatal crashes involved high alcohol levels. To fight drunk driving, state courts may require that prior DUI offenders install devices that prevent impaired drivers from starting their cars.

Honors of 2007

A selective list: medals, awards, ruffles and flourishes of the year

Rock solid *Cast members of the NBC comedy hit 30 Rock celebrate winning the Emmy Award*

NOBEL PRIZES

Chemistry
Gerhard Ertl (Germany)

Economics
Leonid Hurwicz, Eric S. Maskin and Roger B. Myerson (U.S.)

Literature
Doris Lessing (U.K.)

Medicine
Mario Capecchi (Italy), Martin Evans (U.K.), Oliver Smithies (U.S.)

Peace
Al Gore (U.S.), Intergovernmental Panel on Climate Change (U.N.)

Physics
Albert Fert (France) and Peter Grünberg (Germany)

PULITZER PRIZES

Journalism: Public Service
Wall Street Journal

Journalism: Commentary
Cynthia Tucker, Atlanta *Journal-Constitution*

Journalism: Criticism
Jonathan Gold, *LA Weekly*

Journalism: Editorial Writing
Editorial board, New York *Daily News*

Journalism: Editorial Cartooning
Walt Handelsman, *Newsday*

Fiction
Cormac McCarthy (*The Road*)

Drama
David Lindsay-Abaire (*Rabbit Hole*)

History
Gene Roberts and Hank Klibanoff (*The Race Beat*)

Biography
Debby Applegate (*The Most Famous Man in America*)

Poetry
Natasha Trethewey (*Native Guard*)

General Nonfiction
Lawrence Wright (*The Looming Tower*)

Music
Ornette Coleman (*Sound Grammar*)

OSCAR AWARDS

Best Picture
The Departed

Best Documentary Feature
An Inconvenient Truth

Best Actor, Leading Role
Forest Whitaker (*The Last King of Scotland*)

Best Actress, Leading Role
Helen Mirren (*The Queen*)

Best Actor, Supporting Role
Alan Arkin (*Little Miss Sunshine*)

Best Actress, Supporting Role

Gore The former Vice President was awarded the Nobel Peace Prize for his role in educating the public on global warming

Jennifer Hudson *(Dreamgirls)*

Achievement in Directing
Martin Scorsese *(The Departed)*

Best Foreign Language Film
The Lives of Others

TONY AWARDS

Best Play
The Coast of Utopia (Tom Stoppard)

Best Musical
Spring Awakening

Best Revival of a Play
Journey's End

Best Revival of a Musical
Company

Best Leading Actor, Play
Frank Langella *(Frost/Nixon)*

Best Leading Actress, Play
Julie White *(The Little Dog Laughed)*

Best Leading Actor, Musical
David Hyde Pierce *(Curtains)*

Best Leading Actress, Musical
Christine Ebersole *(Grey Gardens)*

EMMY AWARDS

Outstanding Drama Series
The Sopranos

Outstanding Comedy Series
30 Rock

Outstanding Miniseries
Broken Trail

Outstanding Made for TV Movie
Bury My Heart at Wounded Knee

Best Variety, Music or Comedy Series
The Daily Show with Jon Stewart

Best Actor, Drama Series
James Spader *(Boston Legal)*

Best Actor, Comedy Series
Ricky Gervais *(Extras)*

Best Actress, Drama Series
Sally Field *(Brothers & Sisters)*

Best Actress, Comedy Series
America Ferrera *(Ugly Betty)*

GRAMMY AWARDS

Record of the Year
Not Ready to Make Nice, Dixie Chicks

Album of the Year
Taking the Long Way, Dixie Chicks

Regal *Britain's Helen Mirren celebrates her Best Actress Oscar for* The Queen

Song of the Year
Not Ready to Make Nice, Dixie Chicks

Best New Artist
Carrie Underwood

Best Female Pop Vocal Performance
Ain't No Other Man, Christina Aguilera

Best Male Pop Vocal Performance
Waiting on the World to Change
John Mayer

Best Rock Song
Dani California, Red Hot Chili Peppers

Best Rock Album
Stadium Arcadium, Red Hot Chili Peppers

KENNEDY CENTER HONOREES

Leon Fleisher

Steve Martin

Diana Ross

Martin Scorsese

Brian Wilson

NATIONAL MAGAZINE AWARDS

Design
New York

Feature Writing
GQ

Fiction
McSweeney's

General Excellence (by size)
Foreign Policy

New York

Wired

Rolling Stone

National Geographic

ROCK AND ROLL HALL OF FAME INDUCTEES

Grandmaster Flash & the Furious Five

R.E.M.

The Ronettes

Patti Smith

Van Halen

PRITZKER PRIZE, ARCHITECTURE

Richard Rogers (U.K.)

MAN BOOKER PRIZE, FICTION

The Gathering, Anne Enright (Ireland)

Legends keep rocking *Michael Stipe of R.E.M., left, joins Keith Richards of the Rolling Stones and punk-rock pioneer Patti Smith in a jam at the Rock and Roll Hall of Fame induction ceremony*

The Year in Words

It's tempting, but don't blame the media: we're just taking notes

'She gave me a look that only a mother could give a child.'

PRESIDENT GEORGE W. BUSH, *about a glance Queen Elizabeth II gave him at a White House welcoming ceremony during her U.S. visit in May after this verbal slip: "You helped our nation celebrate its Bicentennial in 17 ... in 1976"*

'Thanks for the question, you little jerk. You're drafted.'

JOHN MCCAIN, *Republican U.S. Senator, responding jokingly to a Concord, N.H., high schooler's comment that at 71, McCain might be too old to serve as President*

'I am actually enjoying everything more than I ever have. God hasn't promised us tomorrow, but he has promised us eternity.'

TONY SNOW, *White House press secretary, speaking at alma mater Davidson College in North Carolina. Fighting cancer, Snow resigned his post Sept. 14*

'We're still playing around with the question, Is he black enough? Stop that nonsense.'

MICHELLE OBAMA, *wife of candidate Barack Obama, speaking to black women about his biracial heritage*

'I believe my attendance could divert attention from the purpose of the occasion, which is to focus on the life and service of Diana.'

CAMILLA PARKER BOWLES, *Duchess of Cornwall and wife of Prince Charles, stating that she would not be attending a memorial service for Diana, Princess of Wales, on Aug. 31*

'It is politically inconvenient to acknowledge what everyone knows: the Iraq war is largely about oil.'

ALAN GREENSPAN, *former chairman of the U.S. Federal Reserve, in his memoirs, published in September*

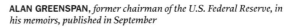

Annals of Law Enforcement

'You get 79 channels here—ESPN!'

CALIFORNIA FELON, *who relocated to a prison in Tennessee, in a state-sponsored videotape shown to inmates in California penitentiaries in an attempt to persuade Golden State prisoners to transfer to jails in other parts of the country*

'It suddenly dawned on me that most people running from the law don't eat out. They order pizza.'

CYNTHIA BROWN, *of the Butler County Child Support Enforcement Agency in Ohio, on her inspiration for placing wanted posters of child-support scofflaws on local pizza boxes*

'We think that by end of the year you will notice a new, fresh look when you are intercepted by one of our men.'

J. MAHAPATRA, *police commissioner of Ahmadabad, India, on a new fabric being developed for the city's police force that is rose and lemon scented*

'Was there an open competition to supply the designs? If so, what on earth do the rejected ones look like?'

BOB NEILL, *2012 Olympics spokesman, after the unveiling of the logo for the London Games, which he condemned as "hideous" and "a waste of money"*

'This isn't the 15th century. You can't go around the world and just plant flags and say, "We're claiming this territory."'

PETER MACKAY, *Canada's Foreign Minister, on a Russian crew's planting a flag on the seabed at the North Pole in order to lay claim to any mineral deposits that might be buried below*

'Some players have psychologists, some have sportologists. I smoke.'

ANGEL CABRERA, *pro golfer, after defeating Tiger Woods and Jim Furyk by one shot at the U.S. Open*

ALASTAIR GRANT—AP IMAGES

'There really is no way to go back and give them that innocence that was taken from them. The one thing I wish I could give the victims . . . I cannot.'

CARDINAL ROGER MAHONY, *Archbishop of Los Angeles, apologizing to the more than 500 victims of clergy abuse in the archdiocese, which agreed to a record $660 million settlement*

'There was only tea and vinegar in the shops, meat was rationed, and huge petrol lines were everywhere. Now I see people on the streets with cell phones, and there are so many goods in the shops, it makes my head spin.'

JAN GRZEBSKI, *a Polish man who emerged from a 19-year coma in April*

'People are at least as smart as goats. Now one of the ways I keep those goats in the fence is I electrified them. Once they got popped a couple of times, they quit trying to jump it.'

TRENT LOTT, *Republican Senator from Mississippi, on how to deal with illegal immigration at the border*

JULIE HABEL—CORBIS

Loudmouths of the Year

JIM RUYMEN—UPI—LANDOV

'I was going to have a few comments on the other Democratic presidential candidate, John Edwards, but you have to go into rehab if you use the word faggot.'

ANN COULTER, *conservative columnist, about the former Senator*

'I'm more of a man than any liberal.'

COULTER, *after her remark about Edwards*

'GENERAL PETRAEUS OR GENERAL BETRAY US?'
Headline of a full-page ad in the New York Times placed by the Democratic group **MOVEON.ORG**

'If this Virginia Tech shooter had an ideology, what do you think it was? This guy had to be a liberal.'

RUSH LIMBAUGH, *conservative radio host, about Cho Seung-Hui, who killed 32 people in the Virginia Tech massacre, in part to take revenge against "wealthy people"*

'Go back to the kitchen. Go in there and make me some bacon and eggs, would you?'

CEDRIC MAXWELL, *Boston Celtics radio commentator, criticizing a female referee during a game; he later apologized*

'Can you provide documented evidence of illicit sexual or intimate relations with a congressperson, senator or other prominent officeholder?'

LARRY FLYNT, *publisher of* Hustler *magazine, in a full-page Washington Post ad offering up to $1 million to anyone willing to provide proof of having an affair with an elected official*

'I couldn't get over the fact that there was no difference between Sylvia's restaurant and any other restaurant in New York City. I mean, it was exactly the same, even though it's run by blacks, primarily black patronship.'

BILL O'REILLY, *conservative media personality, on his Fox News TV talk show*

MARCEL THOMAS—FI MMAGIC—GETTY IMAGES

Nation

A Question of Justice

Evoking memories of the 1960s, tens of thousands of people marched through the streets of tiny Jena, La., on Sept. 20 to protest what they described as a travesty of justice. The case involved a series of racially charged incidents at the Jena public high school, which culminated in the beating of a white student by six teenage black students on Dec. 4, 2006.

All the teenagers, later dubbed the Jena Six, were charged with attempted second-degree murder—very severe charges for a schoolyard fight. Only one of them, Mychal Bell, had been tried as of October 2007; his two convictions were overturned on a technicality, but he was held in jail for 10 months until his bail was posted. Black students charged that the beating was spurred by a series of provocations by white students, including the hanging of nooses, grisly reminders of the South's history of lynching, in a tree at the school. But no white students were charged with misdeeds. The story remained a local issue until it was publicized by black activists in the summer of 2007, spurring the march.

SHARON STEINMANN—THE HOUSTON CHRONICLE—AP IMAGES

General David Petraeus
Can the Army's top counterinsurgency ace solve Iraq?

DAVID PETRAEUS, THE TOP U.S. COMMANDER IN Iraq, is not your old-school, blood-and-guts sort of general. He's an intellectual, a West Point graduate with a Ph.D. in international relations from Princeton and an expert in counterinsurgency. True, the man whose doctoral dissertation analyzed the U.S. quagmire in Vietnam (and who married the daughter of West Point's superintendent) has successfully led soldiers in combat. And he does have his macho moments, famously challenging his soldiers to push-up contests. But he made his reputation more as a communicator and motivator than as a warrior. His record in Iraq prior to taking the top job was mixed. His counterinsurgency efforts in Mosul during the first year of the war succeeded for a time, but his highly publicized effort to train the new Iraqi army in 2004 was not a success.

After Bush put Petraeus, 55, in charge of the war early in 2007, the general changed tactics abruptly, threw a ring of fresh troops around most of Bagh-dad and crimped the flow of explosives into the city, making life there markedly better. The "surge" he led took place in a belt of outposts around the capital, where troops barricaded roads into the city, worked with local residents to flush out insurgents and worked to carve out safe zones where markets and normal life could return. Average Iraqis told TIME in September that Baghdad feels safer; the Pentagon claims sectarian violence in the capital has been reduced, and many Baghdad residents want the surge to continue, though polls show more Americans than ever are wary of the Pentagon's statements on the war.

In September, Petraeus and U.S. Ambassador Ryan Crocker delivered their assessment of the state of play in Iraq to a skeptical Congress. The general's smarts, candor and credibility accomplished at least one of the missions assigned to him by the Bush Administration: holding off a full-scale revolt on Capitol Hill. "I am not a pessimist or an optimist about Iraq," Petraeus said at one point. "I am a realist, and Iraq is hard." ∎

Nancy Pelosi

The Lady of the House charts a course for the center

GOING INTO THE 2006 ELECTIONS, DEMOCRATS HAD failed six times in a row to regain control of the House of Representatives—their worst losing streak since the 1920s. Minority leader Nancy Pelosi recognized that recruiting moderate candidates was the key to ending the slide. When the dust settled, as former House Speaker Newt Gingrich pointed out in his profile of Pelosi for the 2007 TIME 100, 61 Democrats represented districts President George W. Bush had carried in 2004. Another result of the victory she helped engineer: in January 2007, Pelosi, 67, was sworn in as the first female Speaker in U.S. history.

As predicted, the daughter of onetime Congressman and mayor of Baltimore Tom D'Alesandro Jr. proved to be an outspoken leader of the opposition. In April the 11-term representative from San Francisco defied the Bush Administration by travelling to Syria and meeting with President Bashar Assad. Later she contradicted Bush's claim that a planned drawdown of U.S. troops in Iraq meant he was beginning a redeployment. "No, you're not, Mr. President," she reportedly told him in a tense White House exchange in September. "You're just going back to presurge levels."

Pelosi defied GOP predictions that she would be a liberal firebrand, brushing aside calls from the left to launch impeachment hearings against Bush and putting issues she holds dear, like gay rights, on the back burner. Instead, she has embraced the centrist agenda that many believe is the Democrats' best chance for widening their House majority (and capturing the presidency) in 2008. Along the way, she has kept the notoriously fractious Democratic caucus in line—and has occasionally won over more than a few Republican votes. As she said when being sworn in as Speaker, "In this House, we may belong to different parties, but we serve one country." ∎

Arnold Schwarzenegger

His boast: Who needs Big Daddy?

"CAHH-LIFORNIA DOESN'T need to wait for the Federal Government," Golden State Governor Arnold Schwarzenegger proclaimed in May, as he announced a new stem-cell partnership with the province of Ontario, highlighting the $3 billion his state is investing in research the Bush Administration has opposed. "We're showing how powerful a state can be." Presiding over what he calls "the nation-state of California" (which he never fails to remind an audience has the world's eighth-largest economy), the onetime muscleman has also signed the U.S.'s first cap on greenhouse gases, which includes unprecedented fuel-efficiency standards for California cars, and is pushing a universal health-insurance plan. He proved he was a hands-on hero during California's autumn wildfire crisis. And when his appeal to the Bush Administration for help in repairing the precarious levees that protect Sacramento was rebuffed, he pushed through a $42 billion bond issue to move forward. "All the great ideas are coming from state and local governments," he told TIME in 2007. "We're not going to wait for Big Daddy to take care of us."

Clearly, Schwarzenegger doesn't waste time listening to naysayers: the ones who said bodybuilding would never be more than a cultish sideshow, the ones who said a Teutonic hulk with a long name and a thick accent could never be a movie star, much less a Governor. To those who say he cannot be President unless the U.S. Constitution is amended, he offers an undeniable observation: "I like to do everything big." ∎

OSCAR HILDAGO—THE NEW YORK TIMES—REDUX

Michael Bloomberg

A can-do technocrat turns New York City into Bloom-burg

DON'T BOTHER TELLING MIKE BLOOMBERG THAT mayors are supposed to fix the streets and collect the garbage. New York City's chief executive officer is steadily remaking the capital of the world in his own image—and along the way, helping transform national politics. His PlaNYC calls for a 30% cut in greenhouse gases by 2030. It seeks to quadruple the city's bike lanes, convert the city's taxis to hybrids and impose a controversial congestion fee for driving into Manhattan (that last goal may elude him). He also enacted America's most draconian smoking ban and the first big-city ban on trans fats in restaurants. He's so concerned about Washington's neglect of the working poor that he raised $50 million in private money, including millions of his own, to fund a pilot workfare program. He is leading a national crackdown on illegal guns, along with running America's biggest affordable-housing program. Oh, and he also engineered a hostile mayor's-

office takeover of the city's long-troubled schools.

This former Eagle Scout and Wall Street info-tycoon is the unlikeliest of politicians: Bloomberg doesn't seem to crave public adulation, and cares even less for dutiful clichés. After he instituted new restrictions on campaign donations—the tightest in the nation— he was asked if he was being hypocritical, since he had spent more than $150 million of his own money to win two elections. "I would suggest that before anyone runs for office, they should go out and become a billionaire," he replied. "It makes it a lot easier."

In Bloomberg's booming city, test scores and graduation rates are up, crime and unemployment are at record lows, welfare rolls are at a 40-year low, construction is soaring, the budget deficit he inherited has become a surplus, and the city's bond rating just hit an all-time high of double-A. "Yes, I'll fix potholes," Bloomberg told TIME, "but that's not why I wanted this job. I was hired to solve problems." ∎

And They're Off!

The 2008 presidential election was already in full swing early in 2007, as Americans anticipated (and dreaded) the longest race in history. For the record, here are the "starting teams"

Republican candidates, Manchester, N.H., 6/5/07

Tom Tancredo

Age 62

Job Rep., Dist. 6, CO

Pitch The conservative is pro-life and favors a very strong line against illegal immigration

Tommy Thompson

Age 66

Job Former Governor, WI

Pitch The former Health and Human Services Secretary bowed out of the race on Aug. 12

Sam Brownback

Age 51

Job Senator, KS

Pitch A hero to the Christian right, he withdrew on Oct. 19, citing a lack of both funds and support

Mitt Romney

Age 60

Job Former Governor, MA

Pitch The czar of the Salt Lake City Olympics runs for the center. His Mormon faith is a wild card

Rudy Giuliani

Age 63

Job Former Mayor, N.Y.C.

Pitch The ground-zero hero runs on his record of cleaning up New York City and standing tall on 9/11

John McCain

Age 71

Job Senator, AZ

Pitch The Vietnam War hero supports Bush's Iraq strategy and reached out to the religious right

Mike Huckabee

Age 52

Job Former Governor, AR

Pitch The Southern Baptist Minister, a social conservative, won respect as Governor of Arkansas

Duncan Hunter

Age 59

Job Rep., Dist. 52, CA

Pitch Firmly partisan foe of abortion and free trade; former chair, Armed Services Committee

Jim Gilmore

Age 58

Job Former Governor, VA

Pitch Always a very long shot, Gilmore became the first to pull out of the GOP race, in July 2007

A FASCINATING SET OF CIRCUMSTANCES IS DRIVING the dynamic of the 2008 presidential election. In Washington, a Republican President whose approval ratings had long been falling—and who lacked a clear heir apparent—occupied the Oval Office, while on Capitol Hill a Democratic Party rejuvenated by its sweeping victory in the 2006 midterm elections was eager to make up for its misplayed opportunities in the 2000 and '04 elections. Outside the Beltway, polls showed voters were restless and troubled: they were unhappy with the long U.S. occupation of Iraq, concerned over kitchen-table issues like health care and falling house values and said they were increasingly dissatisfied with the overall direction of the country.

Enter the candidates—and, sensing that the wide-open race might just reward the darkest of horses—more just seemed to keep entering, kicking off the earliest start for a presidential contest in U.S. history. At the time this book went to press, two of the candidates had already dropped out and another, Republican Fred Thompson, had entered the contest. The going will get tougher—and the number of debaters fewer—as the big day, Nov. 4, 2008, approaches. By then, these pictures will be fodder for nostalgia. Remember when? ∎

Democratic candidates, Manchester, N.H., 6/3/07

Ron Paul	Mike Gravel	Chris Dodd	John Edwards	Hillary Clinton	Barack Obama	Bill Richardson	Joe Biden	Dennis Kucinich
Age 72	Age 77	Age 63	Age 54	Age 60	Age 46	Age 60	Age 65	Age 61
Job Rep., Dist. 14, TX	Job Former Senator, AK	Job Senator, CT	Job Former Senator, NC	Job Senator, NY	Job Senator, IL	Job Governor, NM	Job Senator, DE	Job Rep., Dist. 10, OH
Pitch So right he has run as a libertarian, he is a strong advocate of reducing the power of Washington	Pitch A strong environmentalist, he has long been an advocate of universal health care	Pitch The respected centrist is a financial expert with 32 years of experience in Washington	Pitch The '04 VP candidate is a strong populist, stressing health care and kitchen-table issues	Pitch A firm centrist, the former First Lady points to her experience and a can-do Senate record	Pitch The charismatic newcomer says he is an agent of change; is a strong foe of the Iraq war	Pitch Former U.S. ambassador to the U.N. and Energy Secretary, he has loads of experience	Pitch The centrist cites his Senate service in finance and on the Judiciary Committee	Pitch The farthest left of the field, he has been an outspoken tribune for workers and the poor

Leading at the Turn

A closer look at the candidates topping the polls early in the race

Hillary Clinton

The state of the Democratic presidential race through much of 2007 was aptly summed up by Lourdes Diaz of Miami, who told TIME in August, "My heart is with Obama, but my brain is with Hillary." Lacking her husband's over-the-top charisma, the former First Lady turned Senator instead capitalizes on wonkish precision, tactical savvy and a record as a smart, engaged public servant. The result is a double-edged sword: voters who are predisposed to dislike her invariably come away from hearing Clinton speak impressed by her competence and command of the facts. But even those who are inclined to support her candidacy find it difficult to connect with her on the emotional level where, polls show, most voting decisions are made. Q: Can her careful calibration win hearts and minds?

DARREN MCCOLLESTER—GETTY IMAGES

John Edwards

The Democrats' 2004 vice-presidential candidate is pinning his presidential hopes on Iowa, a place where he and the voters seem to see eye to eye. Wife Elizabeth's candor about her fight against cancer also impressed voters. Outgunned in two crucial areas— money and media attention—he is hoping to close both gaps with a come-from-behind win that will wrest the Democratic establishment from Hillary Clinton's grip and endow him with some of Obama's inspirational heft. But the stakes in this gamble are high: If Edward's doesn't do well in the early contests in Iowa, New Hampshire, Nevada and South Carolina, he will have little chance in the 20 or so states that vote on Feb. 5. With his poll numbers stuck in third place in New Hampshire, that Iowa caucus becomes a must-win. (As this book went to press in October, Edwards and Clinton were leading polls there.) Q: Can the former trial lawyer sell his populist positions to America's political center?

M. SPENCER GREEN—AP IMAGES

Barack Obama

The Illinois Senator has staked out a role as the candidate of conspicuous candor, unflinchingly telling Democratic audiences what they don't want to hear on issues like military spending, education and Social Security. He is not the first to compete in a Democratic primary as the self-styled truth teller against the party's Establishment and entrenched interests, but his eloquence and charisma have galvanized Democratic voters like no candidate since Robert Kennedy in 1968. One result is Obama's stunning success at fund raising: he pulled in more than $31 million in the second quarter of 2007 alone. Q: Can he convince the party faithful he can win?

CHARLIE NEIBERGALL—AP IMAGES

CHARLIE NEIBERGALL—AP IMAGES

GENE J. PUSKAR—AP IMAGES

Rudy Giuliani

The former New York City mayor (and 9/11 stalwart) says he understands terrorism "better than anyone else running for President," and he talks about it more than anyone else. "What he's selling," says GOP pollster Frank Luntz, "is, 'As dangerous a world as this is, I can make it safer.'" Early on, that pitch was working: Giuliani was the consistent front runner among Republican candidates in most national polls through August, even though his very public record—pro-choice, pro-gay rights, pro-gun control, three marriages—is a turn-off to many Christian conservatives. Q: Can a man with a centrist past sell himself to the party's right wing?

Mitt Romney

The former Massachusetts Governor and honcho of the 2002 Winter Olympics in Salt Lake City is hoping that Republicans will prefer a squeaky-clean Mormon to Giuliani, a pro-choice New Yorker on his third marriage. The good news: Romney is smart and pleasant, and he's rich enough to help his campaign financially. The bad news: his opponents have labeled him as much too smooth and much too willing to change his stripes to suit whatever constituency he is addressing at the moment. Q: Can he stay the course?

CHARLIE NEIBERGALL—AP IMAGES

John McCain

While other Republicans have deftly avoided identifying themselves too closely with the war in Iraq, John McCain has been, if anything, a more forceful advocate for victory than the President. McCain took a spectacular fall early in the year, from established front runner to underfunded underdog. With a newly lean campaign operation, McCain 2.0 hopes to stay alive in the race long enough to merit a second look from donors and voters. Q: Can he hang on?

Fred Thompson

With the GOP in a deep funk, many Republican faithful have concluded that Fred Thompson, the preternaturally avuncular actor and former Senator, is the cure-all for their party's ills. His vague record on the issues seems not to have fazed many voters, but by many accounts his diffidence on the podium and campaign trail has. Q: How long can he continue to tiptoe around divisive issues?

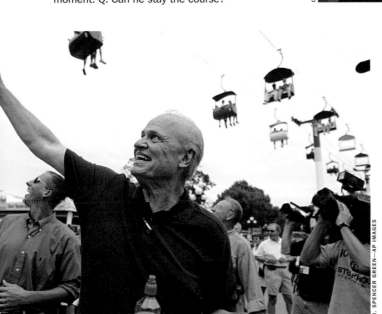

M. SPENCER GREEN—AP IMAGES

Brothers in arms
The President says goodbye to one of his closest allies, veteran political consultant Karl Rove, in August

A Long Sprint To the Finish

George W. Bush vows he won't end up a lame duck, but as the '08 election campaign roars to life, he faces an uphill journey

A YEAR AGO," PRESIDENT GEORGE W. BUSH RECALLED at the April 2007 Radio and Television Correspondents' Association dinner, "my approval rating was in the 30s, my nominee for the Supreme Court had just withdrawn, and my Vice President had shot someone. Ah, those were the good old days." But many truths are told in jest, and his listeners' hearty laughter couldn't quite conceal the fact that if 2006 had been a difficult year for the Bush Administration, 2007 was shaping up to be even more challenging. The White House was beset by a hostile Congress, declining approval ratings, the departure of key staff members— and the early onset of the 2008 election campaign.

Bush had predicted during the 2004 campaign that he had 18 months to achieve his major policy goals, "because after that I'll be quacking like a duck." He now appears to have been mistaken only about the time when the twilight of his presidency would set in. He be-

gan 2007 hoping to emulate Ronald Reagan and (of all people) Bill Clinton, both of whom "restarted" their presidencies during their last two years—Reagan by giving his "Tear Down This Wall" speech and signing a missile-reduction treaty with the Soviets; Clinton by running up a string of budget surpluses and pulling all-nighters working for peace in the Middle East.

The Bush team hoped to reconnect with the American people through two presidential addresses in January. The first announced the troop "surge" that would dominate discussion about the Iraq war for the rest of the year. The second, Bush's penultimate State of the Union address, was meant to showcase a pragmatic President who was both willing and able to work on a robust domestic agenda, even with a Democratic Congress.

Neither speech was the home run that Bush needed to gain traction. Though the American public showed no enthusiasm to commit more blood and treasure to

Iraq, Bush implemented his surge strategy. And his overtures to the opposition on the hot topic of immigration law ended up infuriating his conservative base.

Within weeks of the State of the Union, the President's domestic agenda was robbed of both attention and momentum by a series of scandals—the exposure of substandard conditions at Walter Reed Army Medical Center, the inquiries over Attorney General Alberto Gonzales' firing of seven U.S. Attorneys, and the controversy over his appointee, World Bank president Paul Wolfowitz—that forced the Administration to play defense. Meanwhile, the President found himself not only battling emboldened congressional Democrats over U.S. policy in Iraq but also trying to fend off a rebellion among disenchanted members of his own party on the war. Reliable GOP stalwarts Pete Domenici, John Warner, Richard Lugar and Chuck Hagel all joined Democrats in calling for a change in policy.

On Aug. 13, Karl Rove, the key aide whom critics (with grudging admiration) called "Bush's Brain," announced he was resigning, a sign that the driving energy behind six years of political victories had gone out of the White House, especially on the domestic front. The health-care proposal trumpeted in the State of the Union address seven months earlier was dead on arrival. The proposed immigration overhaul proved to be a reprise of Bush's 2006 defeat on that issue—a bitter pill for the former Texas Governor, who cares deeply about the issue. Worse, Bush lost the trust of conservatives in the GOP base. Much of this failure was laid at Rove's door, even by fellow Republicans. "In politics, nobody was better," Republican operative Richard Viguerie told TIME. "At policy, he was a disaster."

Indeed, the major domestic programs pushed by Rove—the expensive expansion of Medicare, the controversial educational reform program No Child Left Behind, the collapse of Bush's effort to reform Social Security through partial privatization and the vain pursuit of immigration reform—created an uncomfortable climate for the GOP as a whole and especially for the candidates for the '08 nomination. They mentioned Bush infrequently on the stump and didn't endorse his domestic policies, except for his tax cuts. Ironically, the best news for the White House in 2007 came from the least-expected area: Iraq. The surge policy helped to quell violence, reduce U.S. deaths—and buy more time to salvage the Administration's greatest gamble.

Even his critics concede Bush is a fighter. Citing Presidents like Harry Truman, who were once reviled but later revered, he declared he'd continue to do what he thought was right and let the politics take care of itself. He meant it: on Oct. 3 he vetoed an extension of the SCHIP plan, which provides health coverage to millions of U.S. children and which enjoyed broad bipartisan support. On Oct. 17 he said again, "I'm going to sprint to the finish." When his SCHIP veto stood the next day, the Oval Office sprinter didn't seem to be quacking like a duck yet, but he may have been gasping for breath. ∎

All the President's Men

The Bush Administration began 2007 with a strong agenda for domestic policy, but a trio of long-running sideshows diverted White House energy

Alberto Gonzales

The Attorney General battled with Congress over the December 2006 firing of seven federal prosecutors for what critics alleged were political reasons. Testimony in which he claimed not to recall crucial (and relatively recent) conversations hurt his cause, as did a March admission that "incomplete information" had been furnished to congressional investigators by the Department of Justice—and his statement that there was "no express grant of habeus corpus in the Constitution." On Aug. 27 he said he would resign.

I. Lewis (Scooter) Libby

Libby, formerly the chief of staff to Vice President Dick Cheney, was convicted in a U.S. District Court on March 6 of perjury, lying and obstruction of justice on charges related to his role in leaking the identity of CIA operative Valerie Plame. On July 2, President Bush commuted his sentence of 30 months in prison, saying, "I respect the jury's verdict. But I have concluded that the sentence ... is excessive."

Paul Wolfowitz

The militant muse behind the Iraq invasion amassed a legion of enemies who pursued him as he migrated from the Pentagon to the World Bank, promising a war on poverty and corruption. But his campaign sounded hollow when it emerged that Wolfowitz had arranged a $60,000 raise for his girlfriend, a bank employee. As criticism mounted, Wolfowitz was forced to announce his resignation on May 17.

California 911

Massive wildfires ignite broad swaths of Southern California in October, forcing hundreds of thousands from their homes

O N FRIDAY MORNING, OCT. 26, RESIDENTS OF SAN Diego who live near the Pacific coast woke up excited to see something they usually don't welcome: fog. The previous days had brought calamity to their region, so often described as a paradise on earth. Now, after five days of wildfires that charred more than 355,000 acres and destroyed more than 1,400 homes in the San Diego area alone, the weather was mercifully showing signs of change. By evening, the hot desert winds known as Santa Anas were gone, replaced with a cooling breeze more typical for late October.

California's great October wildfires of 2007 were breathed into life by those Santa Anas, winds that ironically begin cold, gathering power and mass in the high desert between Las Vegas and Los Angeles. Air pressure pushes the winds up and over the San Gabriel Mountains, westward toward the Pacific Ocean, until gravity takes hold. The air becomes compressed as it drops, growing hotter and drier, stripping moisture from the ground, accelerating sometimes past 100 m.p.h. as it squeezes through Southern California's many desert canyons.

The punishing gusts of the Santa Anas herald cursed weather, days and nights of devilish heat. Should a fire spark in the dry woodlands surrounding the region's cities and suburbs, the winds become a flamethrower, spreading glowing embers half a mile or more. The Santa Anas have been midwife to the most destructive wildfires in California's history, from the Great Fire of 1889 to the 2003 disaster that blackened nearly 700,000 acres (280,000 hectares) of forest. Lifelong residents of the state know the Santa Anas and dread them. As Joan Didion has written, "The wind shows us how close to the edge we are."

In the autumn of 2007 the people of Southern California were pushed right up against that edge, as wildfires began to ignite overnight on Oct. 20 and spread quickly and relentlessly through the region. "We're in a state of shock right now," Dr. Zab Mosenifar, director of the Cedars-Sinai Women's Guild Pulmonary Disease Institute in Los Angeles, told TIME early in the ordeal, as he prepared for an influx of smoke-inhalation victims at his hospital. "This is beyond thinking."

California's dire situation was worsened by a relatively wet winter in 2004-05, which let trees and scrub grow densely, followed by extremely dry weather, which turned more vegetation into wildfire fuel. The

Sierra H

This is not a drill *Firefighters doing
battle with the Buckweed fire race down
Sierra Highway in Canyon Country,
northwest of Los Angeles, on Oct. 21*

Up in flames *A home burns on Oct. 22 in Poway, Calif., in San Diego County, the region hardest hit by the wildfires*

The Fires by the Numbers

12 Number of separate major fires during the crisis.

14 Number of individuals who died during the disaster. Seven deaths were directly related to the fires; seven others occurred during the evacuation process.

133 Number of people injured; 108 firefighters and 25 civilians.

2,196 Number of homes destroyed by the fires.

3,000+ Number of California prison inmates who volunteered to fight the fires.

8,000+ Estimated number of U.S. firefighters who traveled to California to assist the effort.

14,400 Number of firefighters deployed statewide.

515,267 Number of acres burned in the fires.

900,000+ Number of people evacuated during the crisis.

$1 billion+ Estimated overall property damages caused by the fires.

Source: California State Office of Emergency Services

year 2007 brought the worst drought in Los Angeles' recorded history. Adding to the tinder were those Santa Ana winds, which strike regularly in the autumn but rarely with the power of the 2007 calamity.

In San Diego County, site of the worst fires, people spent a few minutes gathering some mementos before abandoning their houses ahead of the flames, seeking refuge with relatives or friends or even in Qualcomm Stadium, which went from being home of the N.F.L.'s San Diego Chargers to acting as a temporary shelter for more than 10,000 refugees—stirring worrisome memories of the tens of thousands who swarmed to the Superdome in New Orleans in 2005. Hotels filled quickly, highways jammed, and grocery-store shelves ran bare. Some residents learned of the danger through television coverage of the fire. The images of the flames they couldn't yet see out their windows but knew were on the march only added to an atmosphere of terror.

State and federal officials did their best to quell the anxiety of refugees and of people who, at least for the time being, were still in their homes. California Governor Arnold Schwarzenegger was in full combat mode, traveling to the firefighters' front lines, while President George W. Bush, chastened by his Administration's notoriously dilatory response to Hurricane Katrina, declared the region a "major disaster" and promptly dispatched Homeland Security Secretary Michael Chertoff, along with Army helicopters, troops

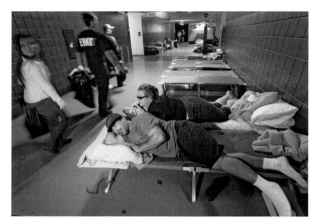

Sanctuary *Evacuees bunk down in Qualcomm Stadium in San Diego on Oct. 24. There were 90-minute traffic jams outside the facility as volunteers arrived to offer food and assistance*

and millions of dollars in federal aid. San Diego city officials even implemented a reverse-911 system with automated warning calls going to residents, urging them to evacuate. This early and aggressive emptying of the region—a hard-earned lesson of the 2003 fires, which left 20 people dead—likely saved Californians' lives, if not their property. "The issue this time is not preparedness," said San Diego City Council president Scott Peters. "It's that the event is so overwhelming."

Then, after blowing fiercely for more than a week, the Santa Ana winds died down, the humidity cranked up, and hundreds of thousands of Californians returned to their homes. By Sunday, Oct. 28, skies were blue and temperatures were in the low 70s. The week's single biggest blaze, the Witch fire in North County, had burned 197,990 acres, destroyed 1,040 homes and was 95% contained. As the good weather continued, the fires were slowly brought under complete control.

Even as the blackened landscape still smoked and popped, the nation was sorting through the equal measures of heroism and folly that accompany such disasters. There was the valiant army of firefighters and other personnel who waded into the flames and slowly beat them back. There was Schwarzenegger, adept at both crisis management and showmanship, who received a general's welcome after the disaster as he tossed the coin to begin the San Diego Chargers game at a spotless Qualcomm Stadium, which only days earlier had been home to thousands of evacuees.

There was the search for arsonists, who are believed to have started at least two of the fires. There was, too, the fumbling FEMA, which, desperate for redemption after the fiasco of Katrina, almost seemed to get it right, until it staged a faux news conference touting its achievements, undermining its comeback campaign. Finally, of course, there are Americans as a whole, a stubbornly homesteading people who never seem to tire of building in the paths of fires, hurricanes and coastal floods. There is little to suggest that the California blazes will break us of that obstinate habit. But there is much to suggest that when the crises do hit, we'll at least be ready to help one another out. ∎

The Wildfire Terminator

When Southern California erupted in flames, the state's action-hero Governor, Arnold Schwarzenegger, was ready for his close-up. He had planned to be with his wife Maria Shriver at a major conference on women's issues sponsored by his office, but when the emergency escalated, he rushed to the front lines with camera crews in tow.

With squinting eyes and frowny mouth, Schwarzenegger greeted firefighters and surveyed the ruins of incinerated homes. He explained his response with his customary candor in a message beamed by satellite to the 14,000 conference-goers back in Long Beach. "The most important thing is, you jump into action as quickly as possible," he said. The public needs to see "that you are a hands-on Governor," that you "take care of the firefighters" and share the pain of people who have lost their homes.

Schwarzenegger drew praise from across the political spectrum for his leadership. An early critic of the state's fire response, Orange County fire chief Chip Prather, later had nothing but accolades for Schwarzenegger. His "personal attention" to firefighters battling the blazes "is inspiring—knowing the guy

Hot seat *The Governor tours a torched region in Lake Arrowhead*

at the top is there with them," Prather declared. California's National Guard Commander Major General William Wade extolled the "coordination and cooperation" in the Schwarzenegger-led effort. L.A. County Sheriff Lee Baca said the fires were a reminder that "this state requires the gubernatorial leadership that you provide." Even U.S. Senator Barbara Boxer, a liberal Democrat, joined in, hailing the Republican Governor's "swift action" in deploying National Guard troops to trouble spots quickly.

The obvious competence of California's emergency response—in stark contrast to the debacle of Hurricane Katrina—was the product of years of training, planning and drills. Schwarzenegger's saga ended the way many of his movies wrap up: with a lot of smoke and wreckage but with the hero stronger than ever. This was one time, however, that Arnold might prefer not to star in a sequel.

Vigil *Students honor their fallen classmates at a memorial service on April 17*

A Killer Stalks The Campus

In the deadliest school massacre in U.S. history, an embittered lone gunman murders 32 people at Virginia Tech University

THE CLASSROOMS AT VIRGINIA TECH, IN BLACKSBURG, were open on the morning of Monday, April 16, at 7, including three that had been closed off on Friday after university officials received a second bomb threat in as many weeks. They had offered a $5,000 reward to anyone who knew anything about the matter and were supposed to meet that morning to discuss security measures to deal with the threats.

But when a 911 call came in at 7:15, it didn't involve a bomb: instead, campus police rushed to the West Ambler Johnston dormitory, where they found Emily Hilscher, 19, and residential adviser Ryan Clark, 22, shot to death. Students told police a gunman had been going from room to room, looking for his girlfriend. Assuming they were dealing with a lovers' quarrel, police secured the murder scene and began gathering evi-

dence. The crime was over and its investigation had begun—or so they thought. But they had committed a grave mistake. Detectives and military people have a saying about their line of work: "Assumption is the mother of all f___-ups."

By 8:25 a.m. top university officials, including the president, executive vice president and the provost, were meeting to discuss the double murder and figure out what steps should be taken. An hour later, a campuswide e-mail went out telling of a shooting, urging caution and requesting that students contact the campus police "if you observe anything suspicious."

Cho Seung-Hui, 23, was the mystery hiding in plain sight, a man who wore a hat and sunglasses inside, a student with no Facebook page—and, seemingly, no face. Talking to him, said English department head Lu-

Hunter and hunted *Students in a locked-down classroom during the second of Cho's murderous rampages communicate with the outside world via cell phone. Right, the psychopath's self-portrait*

NBC NEWS

BREAKING NEWS   LIVE 5:56 ET   MSNBC
S&P ▲ 1.02   'CAL 'OBBY HORSE' ®   ROANOKE T

hibit for days, with its 27 QuickTime videos, its self-portraits of Cho as normal kid, its portraits of Cho as avenger. "I didn't have to do this," he said into the camera. "You had a hundred billion chances and ways to have avoided today," Cho says on one of the videos. "You forced me into a corner and gave me only one option … Now you have blood on your hands that will never wash off." After sending the package Express Mail to NBC in New York City, he headed out the door and walked across campus to Norris Hall, home of Virginia Tech's engineering school. His rampage, put on hold for his publicity needs, now resumed.

cinda Roy, "was like talking to a hole. He wasn't there most of the time." Even students who had lived with Cho knew virtually nothing about him; the simplest conversations—Where are you from? What's your major?—got a monosyllabic response. A "hello" was a big deal. They never heard him talk about weapons or killing or violence—because he never talked at all. "We just thought he was shy," his suitemate Karan Grewal told TIME. It was not until two days after the shootings, on the night of April 18, when NBC News aired the words and images Cho had sent them in the midst of his murdering spree, that these students and everyone else had a chance to see all the ego, the anger and the desire to get even for perceived slights that animated his fury.

But no one was observing Cho at that point. He appears to have gone back to his room in Harper Hall, reloaded his weapons and tucked two knives into his backpack. He had clearly been preparing his NBC ex-

Introductory German was meeting in Room 207, a couple dozen students in their first class of the day, when Cho peered in, as though he was looking for someone. One student thought he looked like a Boy Scout. He was wearing the school color—a maroon cap—and a vest with pockets for his ammunition. When he entered the classroom, he was quiet and purposeful. First he shot instructor Jamie Bishop, 35, in the head. Then he went methodically around the room. Derek O'Dell was hit in the arm; when Cho finally left for the next room, O'Dell and two other students moved to block the classroom door in case he returned—which he did, firing into the door several times before moving on. Cho then moved through three more classrooms in the building and a stairwell, killing 30 more people. Then he shot himself in the face, a final act of deletion.

Norris Hall immediately became a 72,000-sq.-ft. crime scene; federal agents called it the most horrifying they had ever encountered. A federal source said it appeared that as many as "a couple of hundred" rounds had been discharged. They didn't see a wild rampage, a maniac who suddenly snapped; they saw calculation. The gunman's extraordinary effectiveness and, according to witnesses, well-planned, coldly methodical killing suggested someone who had trained himself in "execution style" killing, according to the federal source.

At twilight, the stately, sprawling Virginia Tech campus was littered with broken branches; yellow police tape ribboned through a tree as if the strong gusts of the windy day had tied it there, mourning those who would not be coming back. ■

Medic! *Police carry seriously wounded senior Kevin Sterne from Norris Hall. Sterne survived his ordeal by fashioning a makeshift tourniquet from a cord*

War's Burden

Veteran TIME photojournalist **Anthony Suau** trains his camera on

"YOU GO TO WAR WITH THE ARMY YOU HAVE ... NOT the Army you might want," former Secretary of Defense Donald Rumsfeld once famously told a grunt in Iraq who complained that he and his comrades' vehicles didn't have enough armor to protect them. More than four years into the U.S.

occupation of Iraq and its mission in Afghanistan, the Army Rumsfeld had at the outset of the conflicts has been stretched to its limits by the long struggle, and the costs of the war on the home front are still being felt almost exclusively by soldiers and their families, rather than by the general public.

Tailgating *GIs from the U.S. Army's Third Infantry, Third Brigade, share their last hours in the U.S. with their families at Fort Benning in Georgia*

Hurry Up—and Wait *Grunts get some shuteye before boarding the plane*

The longest march *Soldiers depart Fort Benning for duty in Iraq*

the effects of a faraway war on soldiers and their families at home

To illustrate a cover story on "Why Our Army Is at the Breaking Point," TIME sent Anthony Suau to document the life of soldiers and their families at home. In 2007 half the U.S. Army's 43 combat brigades are deployed overseas, with the remainder recovering from their latest deployment or preparing for the next one. Repeated combat tours have "a huge impact on families," General Peter Schoomaker, the Army chief of staff, told Congress in February. Some 170,000 soldiers have now served multiple tours in Iraq or Afghanistan; they show a 50% increase in acute combat stress over those deployed only once. ■

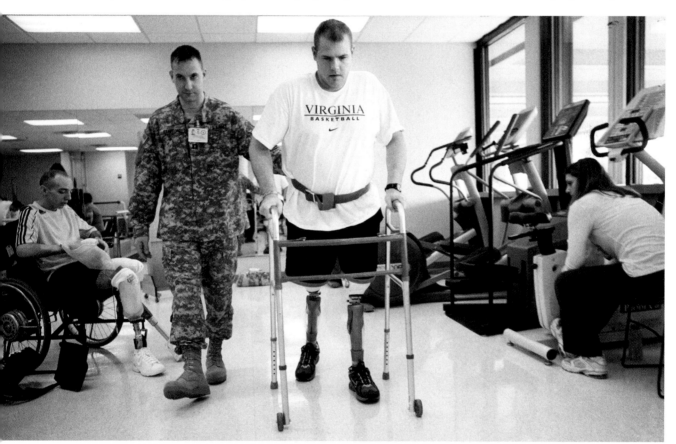

arting over Double amputee Dennis J. Leonard Jr. practices walking on his new prosthetic limbs at Walter Reed Army Hospital

bute Bikers show respect at a soldier's funeral procession in Maryland

Grief *Rachel Guy-Latham, 22, mourns her husband, Thomas Latham, 23*

A Calamity of Nuts and Bolts

A bridge rated deficient for 17 years collapses in Minneapolis, killing 13 and exposing the perils of our unstable structures

WE JUST HEARD THIS LOUD, ALMOST ... THUNDER-ous boom," witness Courtney Jensen would recall later. Parked during the evening rush hour just a few hundred yards from the eight-lane Interstate 35W bridge that crossed the Mississippi River in the heart of Minneapolis, she turned, "and I saw the bridge go down. I couldn't believe ... it's in the river!"

"We were [in] bumper-to-bumper traffic," remem-

bered Gary Babineau, whose pickup was in the middle of the span at that moment. "I was probably going 10 miles an hour. The bridge started shaking. And the whole bridge, from one end of the bridge to the other, just completely collapsed. I thought I was dead. I literally thought I was dead." He recalled the front end of his truck first pointing straight down, then falling into nothingness, then being crushed. "When I got out, it

RICHARD TSONG-TAATARI—MINNEAPOLIS STAR TRIBUNE—MCT—LANDOV

PETER MATTHEWS—POLARIS

Grace under pressure *Far left, the 1,907-ft. bridge is seen just after the collapse; the view is from the east side of the river. Above, a close-up view of rescue workers trying to reach a driver who was thrown into the Mississippi; some people fell as far as 115 ft. Officials hailed emergency personnel, saying lives were saved by their rapid response.*

At left is Jeremy Hernandez, 20, a staff member at a day camp whose courage during the crisis helped save the lives of some 50 children riding on a school bus that came to rest perilously close to a burning semitrailer truck. Hernandez kicked out the rear emergency door of the bus and helped all the children make their way to safety.

was folded in half," he said. "I can't believe I'm alive."

School bus driver Kim Dahl was ferrying about 50 children (including two of her own) back from a field trip to a water park and was nearing the far side of the bridge when the roadway disappeared beneath them. The 30-ft. plunge shattered two vertebrae in Dahl's lower back, but didn't stop her from supervising the evacuation of everyone onboard. "God gave that bus wings to land as safe as it did," she would say a few days later.

The structure collapsed at 6:05 p.m. on Aug. 1, and within minutes emergency personnel and volunteer rescuers converged on the scene. In less than an hour, more than 20 boats were in the waters around the wreckage, while more than 100 police and fire vehicles lined the shore and scuba divers probed the wrecks of submerged vehicles for survivors. The recovery operation took 21 days, as strong river currents and tough weather conditions hampered the searchers. The final tally of victims was 13, far fewer than initially feared.

"We thought we had done all we could," Minnesota bridge engineer Dan Dorgan would later say, explaining the state's strategy of making patchwork fixes on a

structure that carried more than 100,000 cars each day. It later emerged that inspectors had rated the bridge as "structurally deficient" 17 years earlier. The tragedy sent chills through engineers, highway departments, public officials—and drivers—across the nation: although such deadly collapses are extremely rare, about 77,000 U.S. bridges are rated deficient, some 13% of the nation's 596,808 bridges.

Within days the Department of Homeland Security declared that there was no evidence of terrorism in the disaster. The news was welcome but didn't ease minds: in addition to worries of terrorism, Americans now face a different kind of threat, from aging structures across the nation. Infrastructure itself is a matter of homeland security, a concept that President Dwight Eisenhower understood when he started the federal highway system during the cold war. The healthier a locale is before a disaster (or terrorist attack), the healthier it will be afterward. As we learned the hard way in New Orleans, the opposite is also true. Calamities are inevitable, but if we invest in strong levees, roads and rails, their aftershocks may be less painful. ∎

Notebook

A Monster Twister Levels a Kansas Town

A tornado so huge it looked like Satan's wide-tip marker obliterated the entire town of Greensburg, Kans., on May 4, collapsing buildings with winds over 200 m.p.h. Days later, when President George W. Bush arrived to dispense funds and sympathy, he found scarcely a roof still on four walls or a leaf left clinging to a tree. Lumber scraps lay strewn like hay behind a boisterous hayride. Ten people died in Greensburg, at least 60 were injured, and two more people were killed by a separate twister outside the town. Officials estimated some 95% of the town was leveled.

In a scientific triumph, forecasters were able to alert Greensburg residents 20 min. before the monster hit—otherwise far more lives might have been lost. The next day, dozens more tornadoes were sighted in Kansas, but none proved fatal; at least 10 more twisters were seen on May 6.

Mukasey Takes Over

When a tarnished Alberto Gonzales stepped down as Attorney General on Sept. 14, President George W. Bush realized that his nominee to lead the Justice Department must command the nation's respect. His choice: the admired, retired federal judge Michael Mukasey, 66. Members of both parties initially hailed the selection, but when Mukasey balked at condemning some of the Administration's methods of interrogating suspected terrorists—which critics call torture—he lost the support of some Democrats. The Senate Judiciary Committee voted 11 to 8 in his favor, and he was sworn in on Nov. 9.

Election '08: Casting a Wide Net

If you don't recognize the attractive lady at left, check with college students: they'll likely identify her as model Amber Lee Ettinger, better known to Internet users as "Obama Girl." She's the star of a catchy video and song, *I Got a Crush ... on Obama,* that hit the popular YouTube site in June and by the fall had racked up some 3 million viewings. (The Illinois Senator had nothing to do with the video and publicly scorned it.)

As the '08 race for the Oval Office got rolling in '07, more than ever the campaign was being waged in the digital forum of cyberspace. Hillary and Bill Clinton scored a hit with their video send-up of the ambiguous ending to *The Sopranos;* Obama raised $19 million in the third quarter of the year, a good deal of it via the Net; and traffic to political blogs and websites soared. Politics, once the stuff of cliques, is now about clicks.

TOP: ORLIN WAGNER—AP IMAGES; LEFT: GERALD HERBERT—AP IMAGES

NO CREDIT

Notes from Underground

When 12 miners died after an explosion in a West Virginia mine in January 2006, mine owners and federal authorities vowed they would improve both working conditions in mines and rescue operations when disaster strikes. But when six men were trapped by a collapse in the Crandall Canyon mine in northwestern Utah on Aug. 6, attempts to save them proved even more difficult than in the West Virginia tragedy. Ten days after contact was lost with the six miners, as rescuers tried to dig down to the site of the collapse, the walls of their tunnel exploded inward violently, hurling projectiles of rock and coal at the workers. The awful result: two rescue workers and a federal mine inspector were killed, and six more were hospitalized. Mine owner Robert E. Murray called the mountain "evil"; he was accused by mining families of responding slowly. Rescue operations were suspended on Aug. 31.

RICK BOWMER—POOL—AP IMAGES

LAYNE BAILEY—CHARLOTTE OBSERVER—MCT—LANDOV

Nine Die in a South Carolina Blaze

Among the firefighters who charged into the burning Charleston Sofa Super Store in Charleston, S.C., on June 18 were veterans with decades of experience in fighting flames. They sized up the situation and concluded they could rescue trapped employees and beat down the blaze. Then chaos erupted with a flash and, as a witness put it, a "tornado of flames." Nine men perished when the roof fell into the inferno. The technical term for such an eruption of flame is a flashover, the simultaneous combustion of all flammable material in a given area, a state that generally occurs when temperatures in a given space reach 930°F. A memorial service was held June 22; an estimated 30,000 people lined highways to watch a procession of more than 300 fire engines and other vehicles. Some 8,000 firefighters from across the nation traveled to South Carolina to take part in the event.

A Queen Checks in on the Rebels

Happy Birthday, Jamestown! The first permanent British settlement in the New World celebrated its 400th anniversary in 2007 and invited Britain's Queen Elizabeth II to Virginia to join in the festivities. The 81-year-old monarch obliged, spending a day at the site of the historic colony. The monarch was later saluted at a state dinner by President George W. Bush and, in her role as royal railbird, flew to Louisville to take in the Kentucky Derby.

CHUCK KENNEDY—MCT—LANDOV

JIM YOUNG—POOL—AP IMAGES

Scandal at a Veteran's Hospital

In February 2007 the Washington *Post* published two articles by journalists Dana Priest and Anne Hull charging that veterans of the Iraq war were suffering because of the U.S. Army's severe negligence in operating the famed Walter Reed Army Medical Center in Washington. The fallout was swift: top officers were fired, Congress investigated, and federal veterans agencies promised to review all their medical facilities.

World

Pakistan, flash point for extremism

"My martyrdom is certain," Abdul Rashid Ghazi, head cleric of Islamabad's besieged
Lal Masjid (Red Mosque), told the Pakistani press by phone on the morning of July 10.
Hours later, his bullet-riddled body was carted out of the basement of the sprawling
mosque and madrasah, or seminary, complex, where he and scores of heavily armed
militants had battled Pakistani security forces for eight days. For months students
and teachers at the city's madrasahs conducted a Taliban-style vigilante campaign,
raiding video and music shops for promoting "un-Islamic behavior." They abducted
women they termed "prostitutes," set up their own Shari'a court, kidnapped police-
men and terrorized neighboring areas.

On July 3, that defiance erupted into a bloody clash between security forces and
students when authorities tried to cordon off the madrasah complex as part of a plan
to shut it down. The next day, a shoot-on-sight curfew was in force around the area,
and tensions remained high. After government troops finally moved in on July 10, a
massacre ensued. When it was over, more than 50 militants and upward of a dozen
soldiers were dead, along with an unknown number of civilian bystanders. Above,
a rare look inside the mosque's madrasah shows female novices before the tragedy. In
November embattled President Pervez Musharraf put the nation under martial law.

Vladimir Putin
Flexing Russia's muscles

SAY WHAT YOU LIKE ABOUT RUSSIA'S PRESIdent, Vladimir Putin—although you'd be advised to keep it polite—but he has certainly re-established his country's credibility as a great power. Ten years ago, his nation was in disarray; ordinary citizens endured rampant inflation and unemployment, as well as the humiliation of being a former superpower. Then, at the end of 1999, Putin took over. Since then he has ruthlessly reasserted Kremlin control over political life, the media and the energy sector that drives the economy, which has bounced back with a vengeance. His greatest achievement, however, has been to restore Russia's global clout. If predecessor Boris Yeltsin acted the clown on the international stage, Putin has relished playing the tough guy. On his watch, Russia has grown increasingly pugnacious. In 2007, Putin gave speeches that appeared to draw parallels between the U.S. and the Third Reich and said he would train missiles on Europe if America sited a missile defense shield in Poland and the Czech Republic. He resumed long-range bomber patrols far beyond Russia's borders and sent the Russian navy to plant a titanium-encased flag on the seabed beneath the North Pole.

The former KGB agent is by far the most admired politician in the country, and his party won a landslide victory in early December parliamentary elections. Though the constitution requires that Putin leave office in 2008, there is little doubt that his plan is to keep his iron grip on power, whether from an official Kremlin position, or from a country dacha. ■

DANIEL BEREHULAK—GETTY IMAGES

Benazir Bhutto
Can Pakistan survive the murder of a moderate?

O N DEC. 27, 2007, ONLY DAYS BEFORE PAKISTANIS were to elect a new parliament, leading Prime Ministerial contender and anti-terrorism crusader Benazir Bhutto was shot dead during an election rally in Rawalpindi, near Islamabad. According to early reports, Bhutto was shot in the neck and the chest by a gunman who penetrated security and then blew himself up. As many as 20 bystanders were killed in the blast. Bhutto was rushed to a hospital, but she was declared dead at 6:16 p.m. Pakistan time.

Throughout 2007 Pakistan was plagued by a wave of violence that saw hundreds of civilians killed in similar bombing attacks, prompting President Pervez Musharraf to declare a state of emergency. On Dec. 16 he lifted the order, stating that the threat had been contained. But the bombings continued. Just hours before her assassination, Bhutto, 54, met with visiting Afghan President Hamid Karzai to discuss the threat of terrorism against both countries.

The U.S. has long supported a return to power by Bhutto, who served as Pakistan's Prime Minister between 1973 and 1977 and was perceived to be a moderate willing to work with the U.S. She was also seen as a democratic leader who would serve as a counter to the plummeting popularity of Musharraf, who took power in a 1999 military coup. It was thought that a power-sharing deal between the two, in which Musharraf stayed on as president with Bhutto as prime minister, would promote stability in this nuclear-armed power of 165 million Muslims.

Bhutto's return to Pakistan after eight years in exile was marred when a pair of bombs detonated amid a welcome home rally in Karachi on Oct. 18. Despite the clear threat to her life, she continued to campaign at huge outdoor rallies. "I am not afraid," she told TIME in November, "I am ready to die for my country." Pakistan can ill afford to sacrifice the few moderate leaders it has left. Bhutto's death will plunge the upcoming elections into uncertainty and the country further into instability. And that's good news for terrorism. ∎

Nicolas Sarkozy
France's new boss plays tough

SINCE HE TOOK OFFICE IN MAY, THE PACE SET BY French President Nicolas Sarkozy, 52, has amazed—and exhausted—his countrymen. At home, he rammed through reform legislation aimed at encouraging work, cutting taxes, fighting crime and clamping down on immigration. Scolding workers for laziness, he took aim at France's sacrosanct 35-hour workweek. Abroad, he helped break the logjam over the European Union's institutional setup, negotiated the freedom of six Bulgarian medics facing the death penalty in Libya and strengthened Franco-American relations over a vacation lunch with U.S. President George W. Bush.

Welcome to the "Sarko Show." No French President in living memory has made so many unpopular decisions (and stood by them) in so little time: not bad for

the son of a Hungarian émigré aristocrat who was a mediocre student who never fit in. Always the obstinate outsider, Sarkozy embraced Gaullist conservatism as a young man, eschewing the make-love-not-war spirit of the late 1960s. The hyperactive chief executive seeks no less than to overhaul France's soul, which he views as insufficiently rigorous. In his inaugural address he declared his goal was "to rehabilitate work, authority, morality, respect and merit." But by November, the crusader was running into hurdles on three fronts: his 11-year marriage to wife Cécilia ended; youths in Parisian suburbs rioted after two teenagers were killed in a collision with a police car; and workers took to the streets to oppose his tough new policies. They apparently had no use for Dr. Sarkozy's prescription: less *joie* in their *vivre*. ∎

Gordon Brown
In gloom we trust

NOT FLASH, JUST GORDON," CHIMES THE LATEST slogan of Britain's Labour Party. The joke plays off the giddy delight that both the party and the wider British public are feeling at their newfound affection for Prime Minister Gordon Brown, whose principal selling point in the race to succeed outgoing PM Tony Blair in June was continuity, rather than charisma; he offered experience in lieu of Blair's legendary empathy. Large swaths of Labour's faithful viewed Brown, 56, with trepidation. He'd made a good showing of his 10-year tenure as Chancellor of the Exchequer, most agreed, but wasn't he too brainy, too dour to win over the wider public? After all, this son of a minister of the Church of Scotland (Protestantism does not get more powerfully reserved than that) had so excelled at school that he was accepted into the University of Edinburgh at age 16. Even Blair once referred to him as a "great clunking fist."

But Brown's adroit handling of terrorist attacks in London and Glasgow, just days after he took office, turned public opinion around. To be sure, Brown still faces challenges. As the architect of Labour's economic policies, he presided over an economy that racked up an astonishing 58 consecutive quarters of growth. He must continue that hot streak while also raising the quality of public services, particularly the moribund health system. But each of these may play to the stolidity, once his biggest liability, that is now his greatest strength. As Brown told TIME, "I think people are looking to politics not for gestures [but] for a seriousness about addressing the challenges ahead." ■

MURDO MACLEOD—POLARIS

Still on Patrol

The U.S. intervention in Iraq grinds into its fifth year, as the conflict continues in Iraq's streets—and in two governments

"THE SITUATION IN IRAQ IS UNACCEPTABLE TO THE American people," President George W. Bush told the nation on Jan. 10, 2007, "and it is unacceptable to me ... It is clear that we need to change our strategy." With these words, Bush unveiled a new approach to fighting the Iraq war that, depending on the listener's point of view, represented either a bold new gambit that might yet wrest something resembling victory from a campaign that seemed to have lost its way, or a futile last stab against impossible odds.

As the U.S. intervention in Iraq neared its fourth anniversary in March 2007 and the number of Americans killed surpassed 3,000, it was clear to the President that fewer and fewer Americans were buying his argument that the U.S. must "stay the course" in Iraq. The pasting his Republican Party took in the 2006 mid-term elections was one unmistakable sign that his approach to Iraq had become politically untenable. Polls showed that support for the mission was steeply declining. And the recommendations of the bipartisan and widely respected Iraq Study Group, unveiled shortly after the 2006 election, suggested that the effort was becoming militarily and diplomatically unsustainable.

The White House christened its revamped policy the "New Way Forward," but supporters and critics alike quickly began referring to the new strategy as a "surge." It consisted of funneling almost 30,000 fresh U.S. troops into Iraq, concentrating them in key areas—especially the capital, Baghdad—to quell the violent unrest that had brought the factious country to the brink of sectarian and ethnic civil war. To lead the effort, Bush chose the Pentagon's leading expert on counterinsurgency, General David Petraeus, who had overseen a successful effort to pacify the Iraqi city of Mosul.

Tellingly, in 2004, when Petraeus and the unit he commanded, the 101st Airborne Division, were pulled out of Mosul and replaced by U.S. personnel who didn't share his emphasis on winning the hearts and minds of locals, the city descended into chaos within months.

Petraeus adopted a two-fold strategy. First, he sealed off the urban areas targeted by the surge, making it much more difficult for insurgents to move in and out of Baghdad, hindering their ability to mount attacks. Second, he set about building alliances with local leaders who had previously opposed the U.S. Finding that Sunni chieftans in Anbar province (once the epicenter of the insurgency) had no love for the "foreign fighters," many of them Shi'ites, who were helping keep the insurgency alive, he was able to forge partnerships with one-time adversaries.

With the enemy both isolated and divided, Petraeus' gambit began to make progress that surprised even some of his own senior officers. "Usually everybody's shooting at us," one of them told TIME in June. "This is the first time we've had any of them on our side." By mid-year, as the number of Americans serving in Iraq reached a record 160,000, the frequency of attacks in the targeted areas of the country was down significantly, with many fewer Americans being killed each

Vigilant *U.S. soldiers secure the perimeter of the largely Sunni village of Zurah, north of Baghdad, on March 13*

month. "We're not doubling down here," Petraeus told TIME. "We're all in."

But these encouraging signs were, in some ways, deceptive. For beyond the violence in its streets and cities, there was another front in Iraq. Petraeus himself had said from the beginning that a military victory would not be possible in the troubled nation; instead, he argued, the country could be fully stabilized only through a political solution that honored all sides in the conflict: Sunnis, Shi'ites and Kurds.

Even as the surge strategy calmed Baghdad, Shi'ite Prime Minister Nouri al-Maliki's struggling government failed to achieve at least half the 18 benchmarks U.S. diplomats had set for it earlier in 2007. Crucial areas still unresolved included a reduction in the level of sectarian violence (along with elimination of militia control over local security) and political agreement on a national oil law that would equitably divide the country's vast hydrocarbon resources, without which there could be no reconciliation between its bitterly divided ethnic and religious groups. Many U.S. experts remained skeptical that a political deal was still possible among factions that distrusted and despised each other so completely. One last straw: Iraq's Parliament voted to go on summer vacation for a month, angering Americans of all political stripes.

Still, for the first time in recent memory, the situation in Iraq did not seem to be getting worse, and arguably appeared to be getting slightly better. This faint whiff of military progress proved politically invaluable to Bush, as he faced yet another sort of insurgency, this one on the home front: a long struggle by the Democrats who controlled Congress to impose what they called the voters' mandate in the fall 2006 elections to wind down the war and bring the troops home.

In May, Congress sent to Bush's desk a $124 billion military spending bill that arrived with one very large string attached: a requirement to begin bringing U.S. troops home by Christmas. Bush vetoed the bill—it was only the second time in his presidency that he used this power—secure in the knowledge that Senate Democrats had been unable to attract enough GOP support to override his rejection of the measure. Even so, the perceived success of the surge wasn't enough to prevent further Republican defections: in September, Senator John Warner came out in favor of beginning a troop withdrawal by year's end—joining the ranks of Arlen Specter, Richard Lugar, and Chuck Hagel—all of whom expressed varying degrees of doubt and criticism about Bush's Iraq policy throughout the year.

The Democrats responded by passing a measure that month that would have required more time at home for U.S. troops between deployments in Iraq. (Given the length of time the bill mandated between combat rotations, it would have been mathematically impossible to maintain current troops levels in Iraq.) When this measure also failed to muster enough support to override a presidential veto, it was abandoned.

Pals *A U.S. soldier befriends youngsters in Baghdad. Polls show Iraqis want U.S. troops to withdraw but fear the aftermath of an exit*

The surge bought time Bush badly needed, persuading enough lawmakers on both sides of the aisle to await Petraeus' report to Congress, slated for September, before embracing any radical shift in policy. When the general appeared on Capitol Hill, along with U.S. ambassador to Iraq Ryan Crocker, he came equipped with one commodity that the President no longer seemed able to supply: credibility. Petraeus acknowledged continuing problems even as he cited signs of progress. But he summed up by saying, "The military objectives of the surge are in large measure being met," and he warned that "a premature drawdown of our forces would likely have devastating consequences."

Slam dunk, Petraeus. If members of Congress still harbored serious reservations about Iraq (and many of them did), they were nonetheless unwilling to undercut a commander in the field, especially one who seemed to be inching toward success. As TIME analyst Joe Klein wrote, "An optimistic general will trump a skeptical politician anytime." The medal-bedecked West Point man was largely successful in convincing Congress that the surge's increased troop levels should be sustained well into 2008, guaranteeing that U.S. troops would remain on patrol in Iraq for at least another year—and making it very likely that Bush's successor in the Oval Office would inherit the war. ■

Deadly Diyala

Photojournalist **Yuri Kozyrev** travels with U.S. soldiers as they launc

AFTER INSURGENTS TOOK CONTROL OF THE DIYALA River valley 30 miles north of Baghdad in November 2006, the towns and highways in Diyala province and its capital, Baqubah, became increasingly unsafe. Early in the morning of March 24 the U.S. struck back, targeting the insurgents' safe haven of Qubah, a village on the edge of the river valley. TIME photographer Yuri Kozyrev documented the fight that followed: some 200 U.S. troops landed by air and another force entered by convoy, and after brief skirmishes, the streets were secured. Some 16 insurgents were killed in the first few hours of the

Door by door *A distraught Iraqi man and his family gather outside their home as U.S. troops search inside for possible insurgents*

Branded *Soldiers mark civilians' hands to identify locals from insurgents*

Search party *Soldiers hunt insurgents who fled after the U.S. moved in*

surprise attack against an insurgent stronghold north of Baghdad

mission, but the bloodshed continued for several days, and U.S. troops killed 12 more suspected insurgents after some of them were seen triggering roadside bombs against a U.S. convoy. Four American soldiers and an Iraqi child died in one such blast.

Ironically, the battle for Diyala was in part the result of the initial success of the early 2007 "surge" that sent more Americans into Baghdad, as insurgents left the city to seek haven in the countryside. Still, with no stable government in Baghdad, the top U.S. officer in the Diyala region told TIME, "I can kill [insurgents] all day long. It will do no good." ∎

an down! *Colleagues tend to a U.S. soldier who suffered gunshot wounds to the leg and head in a firefight with insurgents in Qubah; he survived*

op wash *Troops shield a fallen comrade from a rescue helicopter's dust*

Guilty? *Troops round up suspected insurgents on March 25 in Qubah*

Pakistan on The Precipice

Late in the year, the assassination of opposition leader Benazir Bhutto threatens to unleash chaos in an already reeling nation

After Return to Arms Musharraf speaks in September. On Nov. 28 he stepped down as army chief of staff

THERE ARE VERY FEW NATIONS IN THE WORLD WHOSE domestic political tremors cause seismic shocks in Washington, but Pakistan is one. The second most populous Muslim nation on the planet—and the only one with a nuclear arsenal—is a key U.S. ally in a deeply unstable region. So U.S. leaders watched with grave apprehension as Pakistan teetered on the brink of chaos in 2007. President Pervez Musharraf, the savvy general-cum-politician who came to power in a 1999 military coup, spent the year battling emboldened Islamic extremists, jousting with two political rivals—former Prime Ministers Benazir Bhutto and Nawaz Sharif—and dueling with Pakistan's Supreme Court.

After months of turmoil and increasingly deadly suicide bombings, Musharraf clamped down, declaring a state of emergency on Nov. 3—a deed many saw as a desperate attempt to cling to power. Musharraf lifted the decree on Dec. 16; only 11 days later, the nation was rocked by the assassination of Bhutto, just days before her party was expected to perform well in elections for a new Parliament, which would have placed her in a strong position to become prime minister, serving with Musharraf in a coalition government.

How is Pakistan ailing? Let us count the ways. After the 9/11 attacks on the U.S. in 2001, Musharraf aligned himself with President George W. Bush, who has consistently called the Pakistani leader one of America's most important allies in the war against terrorism. For years, Musharraf enjoyed acclaim for his reputation for incorruptibility as well as for getting the U.S. to lift the economic sanctions put in place after Pakistan tested its first nuclear bomb in 1998.

But in 2006 Musharraf agreed to a cease-fire in the mountainous area near the Afghan border, allowing religious extremists and militants to regroup. They have since begun infiltrating into more moderate parts of Pakistan. A U.S. National Intelligence Estimate in July 2007 found that since 2005, al-Qaeda had made a comeback in Pakistan, re-establishing training camps and beginning to plot fresh attacks against the U.S. By the time the cease-fire ended in 2007, suicide bombings suspected of being linked to al-Qaeda had become a regular feature of Pakistani life.

The Talibanization of Pakistan has raised fears that a future regime in the country may put Islamabad's nuclear capacity—estimated to number about 80 devices—into the hands of extremists. The militants have launched attacks against Pakistan's cities, including the capital. In July 2007 the historic Red Mosque in Islamabad became the site of a bloody confrontation between government security forces and radical Islamists that touched off a fresh wave of kidnappings,

Power struggle *Protesting lawyers battle police in Islamabad after Musharraf imposed a national state of emergency on Nov. 3*

bombings and other attacks. Months later, within hours of Bhutto's arrival in Pakistan from exile on Oct. 18, some 140 people in the vicinity of her welcoming convoy were killed in a bomb blast.

Yet even as terrorist groups grew stronger, Musharraf seemed to spend more of his time battling the institutions of a democratic society, particularly the nation's Supreme Court, which had begun to challenge the government's extrajudicial detentions and scrutinize potentially corrupt privatization schemes. Chief Justice Iftikhar Chaudhry was the catalyst for the November crisis in Pakistan. The feisty and independent head of Pakistan's Supreme Court was suspended by Musharraf in March 2007 for alleged misconduct. The move against the judge backfired as Pakistan's lawyers and middle-class moderates, many of whom had once supported Musharraf as a bulwark against extremism, took to the streets in a series of massive protests, and Musharraf's popularity plummeted. In July 2007, the Supreme Court reinstated Chaudhry.

Musharraf's grip on power also came under attack from ancient political foes. When one challenger for the presidency, Sharif, attempted to enter the country in September, Musharraf sent him packing within hours. Musharraf agreed to a U.S.-approved deal that cleared the way for Sharif's rival, former P.M. Bhutto, to return home from exile in Britain and Dubai on the understanding that Musharraf would step down from his army job and then serve another five-year term as President, with Bhutto as Prime Minister.

But by early November, the Chaudhry-led high court seemed set to rule that Musharraf's Oct. 6 re-election, was unconstitutional. The parties of Bhutto and Sharif had boycotted the balloting. On Nov. 3, facing his most serious political challenge in eight years, Musharraf declared a state of emergency, suspending the constitution, sacking the most uncooperative judges, detaining Chaudhry, blacking out the independent news stations and sending security forces into the streets to keep down protests. Many judges, as well as Bhutto, denounced the move as undemocratic. Led by lawyers, moderate Pakistanis took to the streets in massive protests. Many noted that Musharraf spared the nation's Islamic extremists in the clampdown.

After an initially hesitant response, President Bush challenged Musharraf on Nov. 7 to set a date for free elections and to "take off your uniform." The next day Musharraf, who has received $10 billion in U.S. aid since 9/11, declared he would hold parliamentary elections early in 2008. He resigned his military commission on Nov. 28 and allowed both Bhutto and Sharif to resume their pursuit of electoral power. For a few days near the end of the year, it seemed as if Pakistan was on a road to stability. But with the Dec. 27 assassination of Bhutto, the two-time former P.M. who commanded the allegiance of many of the nation's poorest citizens as well as many of its more educated moderates, Pakistan was once again teetering at the precipice of chaos. And in 2008, no nation on earth—especially one that is a nuclear power—is an island. ∎

Gaza, Stripped

Palestinians wage a deadly civil war as Hamas militants rout the centrists of the Fatah party and take over the Gaza Strip

A PUBLIC ATTEMPT AT SUICIDE IN THE STREETS." Thus Palestine's most revered poet, Mahmoud Darwish, described the events in Gaza in a single, shattering June week in 2007, when forces loyal to Palestinian Authority President Mahmoud Abbas engaged in a ferocious battle with Hamas militants. The rush of events concluded with the rout of Abbas' moderate Fatah party and Hamas' takeover of the territory. The stage for this fratricidal conflict was set in 2005, when Israel's Prime Minister, Ehud Olmert, handed Gaza over to the Palestinians, evicting more than 9,000 Jewish settlers in the process. The evacuation of the tiny (140 sq. mi.) Gaza Strip, a beachfront slice of sand dunes and concrete jungles that is home to about 1.5 million Palestinians, was rolled out as the first step in Israel's "disengagement" from the occupied territories. It was to be followed by withdrawals from the larger, more populous and more historically and strategically important West Bank territory on the Jordan River.

Olmert's government hoped that pulling out of Gaza would give Israel a breather from terrorist attacks; instead it accelerated a downpour of rockets into Israel from Hamas and other militant factions in Gaza, souring Israeli officials on giving up any more ground. The plans for disengagement from the West Bank were shelved in 2006. In Gaza, where peace was no longer guaranteed by Israel, tensions rose steadily between the two bitter foes. Fatah's Abbas, 72, is a moderate secularist who has been the titular leader of the Palestinians since the death of Yasser Arafat in 2004 and is willing to restart the peace process. Hamas, led by Ismail Haniya, 44, is religiously inspired and far more militant' it receives significant support from Syria and Iran.

Early in 2007 Hamas and Fatah fighters brawled for power in Gaza's streets, and on June 10 the shooting erupted into a climactic, vicious battle. The fighting between the Palestinian factions, long bitter rivals, reached new depths of savagery, as gangs tossed enemies alive off 15-story buildings, shot one another's children and burst into hospitals to finish off wounded foes lying helplessly in bed. But the Hamas fighters were better organized and more highly motivated than those of Fatah: they didn't so much destroy the Fatah forces as cow them into surrender. Only 5,000 of the

45,000 men on Abbas' payroll actually put up the pretense of a fight. Many top Fatah commanders deserted their men, fleeing either on foot to Egypt or aboard a small armada of fishing boats. The final death toll was estimated to be in the hundreds on each side.

When the shooting stopped, on June 15, Gazans flocked to the beach to celebrate an end to the turmoil—or dashed to the bazaar to stock up on emergency supplies, certain that Israel would close the borders, denying them access to the outside world. They were prescient. Israel soon blockaded almost all shipments, except for basic humanitarian supplies, and halted most exports. The blockade is part of an Israeli and U.S. strategy that seeks to isolate Hamas in the hope that Palestinians will turn away from its Islamist leaders and embrace Abbas.

As of mid-October, the plan hadn't gained a foothold. Now free to govern as they please, Hamas leaders quickly set about building popular support and a military capability that may outlast the international blockade. Still, Gaza's economic woe is immense: with unemployment at around 44%, some 80% of Gazans rely on food aid provided by U.N. agencies.

As the smoke cleared, the rule of law returned to Gaza, just two months earlier one of the most dangerous places on earth. Within a week of the takeover, crime, drug smuggling, tribal clashes and kidnappings had largely disappeared. The newfound peace helped cement popular support for Hamas.

In late November, Ehud Olmert and Mahmoud Abbas shook hands as President Bush stood by, at a peace conference in Annapolis, Md., sponsored by the U.S. The two leaders announced an agreement to begin negotiating a peace treaty, declared they would complete the treaty by the end of 2008, and put the U.S. in the po-

Incoming *A man carries a Palestinian boy wounded when Israeli and Hamas factions in Gaza engaged in rocket duels in May*

MAJED HAMDAN—AP IMAGES

SAIF DAHLAH—AFP—GETTY IMAGES

sition of judging whether they complied with their commitments. It was the first step forward in peace negotiations between the two parties in seven years. But as the leaders grinned for the cameras, a crowd of 100,000 people gathered in Gaza to proclaim their opposition to reviving the peace process, a clear signal of the barriers that stand in the way of peace. ■

Hostage *As Gaza burns on June 15, Fatah militiamen in the West Bank take a hostage; an Islamic court judge affiliated with Hamas, Saleh Frayhat*

Mass Production

In China, photographer **Edward Burtynsky** captures a surge of industrialization that seems to turn workers into widgets

CHINA IS TRANSFORMING ITSELF PERHAPS faster than any other nation on earth, including its Asian neighbor, India. As the People's Republic continues its unusual odyssey, swapping identities from failed socialist utopia to swaggering capitalist giant, some 100 million people have abandoned farming villages for cities. Yet the ancient Chinese cultural feeling for mass movements, for finding one's identity in the "we" as well as in the "I," seems to have remained firmly in place, as these photographs show.

Despite the economic boom for some, TIME's Michael Elliott noted, China remains largely a poor nation, an environmental dystopia where corruption is endemic and growing, where the number of workers far exceeds the number of jobs, and whose leaders are primarily concerned with maintaining stability in the face of the workers' growing complaints. ∎

Roll call *Workers line up for the morning pep talk at the Cankun factory in Zhangzhou*

Pierce work *Some 330,000 chickens a day are converted into shish kebab at the Deda plant north of Beijing, near the North Korean border*

Chow time *Meal breaks that last 20 min. break up the 10-hr. workdays at Younger Textiles in the seaport city of Ningbo*

Hang time *Factory dormitories like this one in China's booming southeast, near Hong Kong, can house up to 1,000 employees*

Notebook

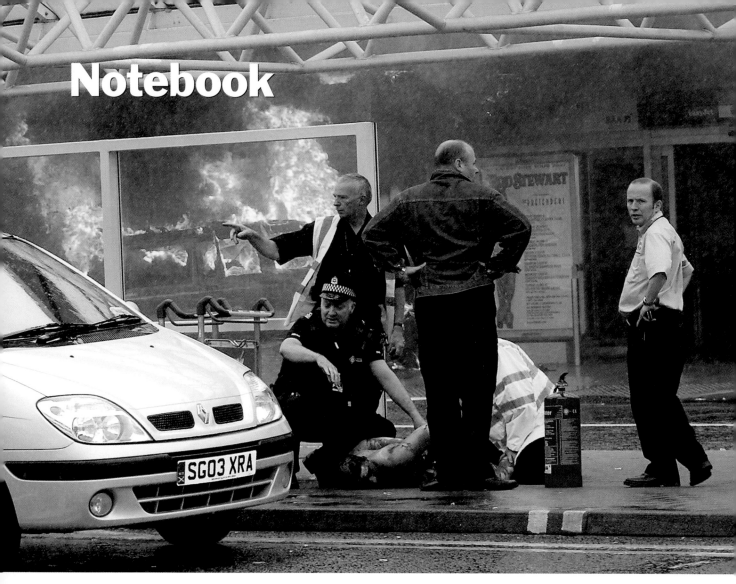

The U.K. Battles Terrorism in the Summer

The United Kingdom weathered several close brushes with terrorism in 2007. Just before 2 a.m. on June 29, police discovered a metallic green Mercedes filled with containers of fuel, cylinders of gas and a pile of nails outside the Tiger Tiger nightclub in London, not far from Piccadilly Circus, a major tourist haunt. About the same time, parking authorities discovered a blue Mercedes containing a similar cocktail of matériel. The very next day, a green Jeep Cherokee filled with gas cylinders and fuel blasted through the check-in entrance of Glasgow Airport in Scotland and burst into flames, above.

"The one overwhelming thing was that [the attacks] defied all of our assumptions," says Peter Neumann, director of the Center for Defense Studies at King's College in London. Among the surprises was the profile of the would-be bombers: five of the eight suspects arrested in the car-bombing cases were doctors, and most of them had worked for the U.K.'s National Health Service. One of those arrested was originally from Iraq, two were from Jordan, two from Saudi Arabia, two from India and one from Lebanon. The two men in the Jeep that smashed into the airport were Bilal Abdullah, a British-born Muslim doctor of Iraqi descent, and Kafeel Ahmed, an Indian-born Muslim. Ahmed suffered severe burns and died on Aug. 2. A note found in the vehicle indicated that both men had intended to die during the Glasgow attack.

Turkey: Tilting Away from the West?

Perched between Europe and Asia, Turkey remains torn between two worlds. In July moderate Prime Minister Recep Tayyip Erdogan was re-elected in a landslide, but Turks tilted east by electing strongly pro-Islam Abdullah Gul as President. In October, above, Turks rallied against a U.S. congressional proposal to label the slaughter of Armenians by Turkey early in the 20th century "genocide." The same month, Turkey threatened to send troops into northern Iraq to battle Kurd rebels filtering into Turkey.

Iran's Divided Identity

With a man Americans love to hate, Mahmoud Ahmadinejad, as its President and a group of secretive mullahs under Supreme Leader Ayatullah Ali Khamenei running the country, it's easy to assume that Iran is a nation of uniformly extremist Islamists. But that's not the case, as several incidents in 2007 made clear. On June 26, disgruntled citizens rioted in Tehran after the government suddenly announced it would begin to ration fuel; the protests spread across the nation but were soon quelled. (Iran is one of the world's largest oil exporters, but its refining capacity is so poor it is forced to import gas.) Another surprising event: the TV airing of a government-sponsored, 22-part series on the Holocaust in September; Ahmadinejad is a notorious denier of the Holocaust. The incidents indicated the divisions in Iranian society, where many people remain firmly pro-West.

AP IMAGES

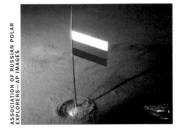

ASSOCIATION OF RUSSIAN POLAR EXPLORERS—AP IMAGES

Squatter's Rights?

The summer of 2007 saw something new under the sun: for the first time in recorded history, the Northwest Passage across the top of the world was ice-free all the way from the Pacific to the Atlantic. The Arctic ice cap's loss through melting this year was 10 times the recent annual average, amounting to an area greater than that of Texas and New Mexico combined. As the race to exploit the region's natural resources also heated up, a Russian-led team descended to the seabed on Aug. 2 and planted a titanium Russian flag directly on the North Pole.

It's All About the (Fake) Benjamins

Below, currency experts in Tokyo examine U.S. $100 bills to determine if they are fake, using a blow-up of an authentic bill as a reference. As counterfeit bills flood Asia, a 2007 TIME investigation reported that a Pyongyang agency known as Bureau 39 is the headquarters of a criminal enterprise that is owned, overseen and operated by North Korea's government and that stretches across Asia and is gaining footholds in Russia, Europe and the U.S. Among its illicit activities: the production and trafficking of opium and heroin and the manufacture and sale of billions in counterfeit cigarettes and U.S. currency. North Korea's estimated total take from such crimes: $1 billion a year.

KAZUHIRO NOGI—GETTY IMAGES

SHAKIL ADIL—AP IMAGES

Pakistan: Ever More Precarious

Benazir Bhutto's triumphal homecoming on Oct. 18, after 8 years in self-imposed exile from Pakistan, didn't last very long: hours after her plane landed, two suicide bombers struck her cavalcade. The former prime minister wasn't harmed, but 136 people died. Bhutto accused Pakistan's government of complicity in the attack: suspects included General Pervez Musharraf's regime; Pakistan's strongly Islamist security agency; and Al Qaeda and pro-Taliban elements within the country. It was only the most spectacular of dozens of bombings in Pakistan throughout 2007, raising ongoing doubts about the future of a volatile nation that has nuclear weapons and is a key U.S. ally in the region.

Society

Parking Space Odyssey

Wolfsburg, Germany, was founded by Adolf Hitler's National Socialist Party in 1938 as a factory city, where Hitler's dream of a Volkswagen (people's car) could be realized. But that was then—and today, Wolfsburg, still the home of Volkswagen, is also the home of the Autostadt, an expansive theme park that celebrates all things VW. Think Disneyland for the Beetle, the Polo, right, the Bentley, the Lamborghini and other marques in the VW stable, each of which is celebrated in its own futuristic pavilion. In July 2007, the massive VW factory adjacent to the Autostadt opened two towering glass parking garages, each 20 floors high and capable of housing 800 new vehicles, which are hoisted into position by a hydraulic lever arm. Buyers can watch as their new car is retrieved from the vertical warehouse—or catch the spectacular view by hitching a ride in an all-glass viewing pod.

Rupert Murdoch
An old-school media tycoon snaps up another trophy

WHAT MAKES A 21ST CENTURY MEDIA MOGUL pay $5 billion for a 19th century newspaper? Others looked at the *Wall Street Journal* and its parent company, Dow Jones, and saw a sagging property that over the years had misplayed juicy opportunities to sell its valuable financial data in the digital arena. Murdoch saw a world-renowned (if economically stagnant) newspaper with a thriving subscription-only website. He also saw the engine of a global, interactive, multiplatform financial network that could drive his upcoming Fox Business Channel, power up his 24-hour Sky News channel in Europe and fuel a still inchoate group of online financial services. His plans for the business channel, which will compete with CNBC, made spending $5 billion for Dow Jones "an easy justification," Murdoch said. "It

almost ensures the price is worth paying." He went on to jest that he paid $60 a share, "plus vitriol."

The onetime outsider, an ink-stained interloper who started in 1953 with a single paper in Adelaide, Australia, had succeeded in adding capitalism's daily chronicle to an empire that comprises the Fox movie studio and television network, satellite TV systems in Europe and Asia, more than 100 newspapers and a fast-growing Internet division that includes MySpace, the massively popular social networking site.

Murdoch is often seen as a hard-line conservative who keeps a tight grip on the strings of his editorial marionettes. But he is also the most gifted opportunist in his business, a visionary who has consistently been able to see around the corner. Love him or hate him, at age 76, he's still at the top of his game. ■

Wesley Autrey

A hero declares, "We got to show each other some love"

FOOL, YOU THE ONLY ONE HERE," WESLEY AUTREY remembered thinking to himself on Jan. 2, as he jumped onto New York City subway tracks to help a man having a seizure, who had fallen into the path of an onrushing train. "You got to go in there." So Autrey sprinted forward, pushed 20-year-old film student Cameron Hollopeter into a 21-in. drainage trough between the rails, then laid on top of him, shielding the younger man with his body as the train rumbled over them, clipping Autrey's hat. Said Autrey to Hollopeter: "Sir, I don't know you and you don't know me, but please don't move."

Soon the whole world knew Autrey, a 50-year-old construction worker, and vied to hail the courage of the "Harlem Hero." President George Bush invited him to the State of the Union address; the U.S. Senate passed a resolution in his honor. Donald Trump sent him a check for $10,000 (and wrote his entry for the 2007 TIME 100); Chrysler handed him the keys to a new Jeep Patriot. The single father of two young girls jetted to the Super Bowl, took his daughters to Disney World, received season tickets to Nets games and was a guest star on network TV shows. Quite a windfall for a man who said simply, "What better way to start out the new year than to save somebody's life?" But there was one gift he probably could put to good use: New York City's Metropolitan Transportation Authority offered him a year of free rides on the subway. ■

RUDY ARCHULETA—REDUX

The Rev. Peter Akinola
A Nigerian cleric threatens to divide a global church

THE ANGLICAN COMMUNION IS A 400-SOME-YEAR-old, 78 million-member fellowship of churches that the British Empire seeded around the globe. Now it may be falling apart. If it does, Peter Akinola, the Archbishop of Nigeria, will have been a catalyst, even if he does not end up prince of one of the pieces.

Akinola, 63, has been a harsh critic of the Episcopal Church, the Anglicans' U.S. branch, since it elected the openly gay Gene Robinson of New Hampshire a bishop in 2003. The Communion's current disarray bears Akinola's imprint. When Anglicanism's 38 primates presented the Americans with demands for a retreat on gay rights and a direct Communion say in Episcopal governance at a tense meeting in New Orleans in September, the Anglican leaders were echoing Akinola's hard line.

Schism looms. In one scenario, Anglicanism's conservative southern provinces may reject church leader Rowan Williams, the Archbishop of Canterbury, as too liberal and chose their own leader—perhaps Akinola. A step in that direction was taken in December 2006, when Akinola helped found the Convocation of Anglicans in North America (CANA), which folded 15 conservative Episcopal congregations in Virginia into his thriving African archdiocese 5,400 miles away. The move, which flouted ancient rules about stealing other bishops' sheep, effectively created a competing Anglican body on U.S. turf.

Akinola's extreme positions (he has said that God regards homosexuality as the equivalent of humans' having sex with animals) have slimmed his chances of becoming the Archbishop of Canterbury of the conservatives. But if he succeeds in dividing his church, he could be the Luther of the Anglicans. ■

Drew Gilpin Faust
A respected female academic is Harvard's new boss

YES, IT TOOK 371 YEARS, BUT WHO'S COUNTING? On Feb. 11, Harvard University named its first female president, Drew Gilpin Faust, 60, a Civil War scholar and dean since 2001 of the Radcliffe Institute for Advanced Study. Faust, whose mother once warned her, "This is a man's world, sweetie, and the sooner you learn that, the better off you'll be," ascends to the most influential job in U.S. academia. After former president Lawrence Summers caused an uproar in 2005 by suggesting that the issue of whether gender differences might explain why few women excel at science was worth study, he asked Faust to head an effort to recruit, keep and promote women at Harvard. Evidently she warmed to the assignment.

Faust, who spent her first day on the job hosting an ice cream social in Harvard Yard and sending an e-mail to students and faculty that spoke of "bridging our differences," has a lot on her plate. Her job entails placating an unwieldy and ego-driven faculty, keeping the university's 11 separate colleges and institutes (which are largely independent and often competitive with one another) on the same page and keeping a Harvard education relevant in today's world. She also must direct a multibillion-dollar fund-raising campaign and plan for a new adjunct campus. And she has vowed to make the arts more central to Harvard's identity. Faust is also expected to find a way to assist more lower- and middle-class students who can't afford Harvard's stratospheric tuition. Too much for one savant to handle? Call it a Faustian bargain. ∎

ERIK JACOBS—THE NEW YORK TIMES—REDUX

Veggie burgher *Ted Blomgren is the top hand at Windflower Farm, a Community Supported Agriculture farm that sells its produce to a syndicate of local buyers*

Home Cookin'

More shoppers in search of the best food (and the best future for the planet) are choosing to think globally and eat locally

WHAT'S FOR DINNER? AS MORE AMERICANS TRY TO eat better, nearly a quarter of shoppers now buy organic products once a week, up from 17% in 2000. But for food purists that's so 2002: "local" is the new "organic," the new ideal that promises healthier bodies and a healthier planet. Many chefs, food writers and politically minded eaters, outraged that "Big Organic" firms now use the same industrial-size farming and long-distance-shipping methods as conventional agribusiness does, are following the lead of Columbia University nutritionist Joan Dye Gussow. As she wrote in her 2001 memoir, *This Organic Life,* Gussow's commitment to eating locally "is probably driven by three things. The first is the taste of live food; the second is my relation to frugality; the third is my deep concern about the state of the planet."

Homegrown helpings *Sous chef Richard Huber grills squash at Google's in-house restaurant, Café 150, which serves only local fare*

One way to look at the issue is to ask, Which is the better fruit—an "organic" apple or a locally grown apple? The answer, it turns out, invites many other questions: What's the most efficient way to grow food for all? Should farms be big or small, family or corporate-run? What tastes better? And how much petroleum was used to ship those Chilean grapes to your table?

One indicator of the new trend is the grocer more and more Americans trust to provide the best food available, Whole Foods Market. Whole Foods now has 190 locations, from Tigard, Ore., to Notting Hill in London. And it's expanding rapidly. Its 2007 acquisition of Wild Oats Markets Inc. will add an additional 112 locations in North America. Already, many Americans have come to see Whole Foods as the repository of both their dietary hopes and fears—the place we can buy not only organic arugula but a decadent chocolate bar too.

Whole Foods began pushing local products more aggressively in the summer of 2006. In stores, placards exhort customers to BUY LOCAL, and cash registers show photos of area farmers. But there's room for improvement. Even in verdant summertime, the vast majority of products sold at Whole Foods (fresh or otherwise) isn't from local farms. Of the roughly $1 billion in produce Whole Foods sold in 2006, 16.4% came from local sources, up from 14.9% in 2005. Saying it wants to increase its percentage of local produce, the company announced a $10 million loan program for local farmers in 2006.

Another leader in the local-food movement is Internet search sensation Google. One of the new cafeterias at its Mountain View, Calif., campus, Café 150, serves only food originating within a 150-mile radius—the famed Salinas Valley region, which boasts a glorious fund of farms,

ranches and fisheries. As one of the most successful companies of the era, Google can afford not only to pursue such a whimsical culinary ideal as total locality but also to do so in the form of a snazzy fine-dining restaurant. Founding chef Nate Keller manages to serve more than 400 purely local meals a day by planning his menus the way preindustrial cooks did, according to whatever local vendors offer that day. Restaurants from Cinque Terre in Portland, Maine, to Mozza in Los Angeles are following suit.

Another way local-food advocates are finding the homegrown fare they crave is by investing in the farm shares run by Community Supported Agriculture programs, in which consumers help support a local farm, like Ted Blomgren's Windflower Farm in upstate New York. Early in the season, members pay a farmer a lump sum. Each week or perhaps once a month in the winter, he delivers fresh vegetables (and, for more money, items like fruit, eggs and flowers) to a central location. One drawback: you don't choose what the farmer grows. He does. You might get lettuce one week, then none for several weeks after. Also, you're locked into purchasing a fixed amount of food each week. The benefit: the food is affordable and phenomenally fresh.

So ... local or "organic"? When asked years ago whether she preferred butter or margarine, Joan Dye Gussow famously remarked, "I trust cows more than chemists." Like Gussow, more and more Americans who trust local farmers more than industrialized agriculture are deciding: you are where you eat. ∎

Cooped up *Nathaniel and Jacob Blomgren are up with the chickens, collecting eggs at the family's upstate New York farm, 185 miles from New York City*

Flashbulb Food

DAN STEINBERG—AP IMAGES

Red carpets, white lies, black marks and purple prose: tabloid headlines covered a spectrum of celebrity behavior in 2007 but, as always, delighted most in accentuating the negative

SVEN KAESTNER—AP IMAGES

"Posh and Becks"

Let's see: there's Tom Cruise and Katie Holmes at left, above, and Will Smith and wife Jada Pinkett-Smith at right. But who are the new faces? Why, it's the Immigrants of the Year, soccer icon David Beckham and wife Victoria, the once-and-future Posh Spice. The stage-managed fanfare over their arrival in L.A. didn't quite take.

The McCanns

Their tragedy took a strange twist: after the 4-year-old daughter of Britons Gerry and Kate McCann went missing during a family vacation in Portugal, the case attracted massive worldwide publicity. Then Portuguese police identified the parents as possible suspects. Madeleine McCann remained missing at press time.

Phil Spector

The producer, famous long ago for his driving and florid "Wall of Sound" pop hits, went on trial for second-degree murder in the 2003 death of B-movie actor Lana Clarkson. After deliberating for 12 days, the jury said it couldn't reach a verdict, and the judge declared a mistrial.

O.J. Simpson

On Sept. 16 the onetime football star was arrested in Las Vegas and charged with robbery with a deadly weapon and several other felonies in what is alleged to have been a commando raid staged by a clutch of geezers to recover some of O.J.'s personal sports memorabilia.

The Nation's Fixation: Bad Girls

Americans remained obsessed with misbehaving pop-culture princesses in 2007, as their exploits provided fodder for a celebrity-scandal media machine whose 24-coverage of the stars' misdeeds was both ugly and unavoidable

Lindsay Lohan

Lohan, 21, crossed some sort of line in 2007: her behavior was so reckless it was clear that she was at the mercy of her worst impulses. The once promising star dropped out of several film projects, was arrested twice and went through at least three rehab programs for substance abuse.

Amy Winehouse

When your biggest hit is called *Rehab* and you sport a tattoo of a naked gal on your arm, you've made the Bad Girls Club! At only 24, the British R&B singer kept tabloids busy covering her sudden marriage, hospitalization, wild behavior and alleged bulimia and drug abuse.

Paris Hilton

After pleading no contest to a 2006 arrest for driving under the influence of alcohol, the hotel heiress, 26, racked up two more traffic offenses early in the year and served 23 days in a Los Angeles County jail. Above, her effigy sports jailbird duds at Madame Tussauds.

Britney Spears

The pop singer, 26, was hoping for a comeback in 2007 but ran into big trouble in her career and her personal life. She was charged with hit-and-run driving without a license in an August incident, and in October a judge granted custody of her two children to ex-husband Kevin Federline. On Sept. 9 she opened the MTV Music Video Awards, left, with a performance so bad it left critics and fans aghast.

iPhone, iSaw, iConquered

Apple's Steve Jobs and Nintendo's Shigeru Miyamoto blaze
the trail for a new era of dazzling cell phones and video games

THE RACE FOR GADGET OF THE YEAR ENDed a bit early in 2007, when Steve Jobs introduced his company's latest creation at the annual MacWorld Exposition in San Francisco on Jan. 9. Jobs, the masterly pitchman who long ago iced his claim to being the P.T. Barnum of the digital revolution, confirmed months of rumors by showing off the iPhone, Apple's bid to transform the ubiquitous, signature communications device of our time, the cell phone.

Jobs put the slim, sleek gizmo through its paces—surfing the Net, downloading music wirelessly from Apple's iTunes store, reading the New York *Times*, resizing pictures with his fingertips, sending text messages using the device's nifty virtual keyboard and, uh, making a phone call or two. Suddenly, every other cell phone on the planet seemed as cutting-edge as a Model T.

On June 29, when the iPhone went on sale, long lines formed outside Apple stores across the globe: without question, Jobs had another iPod-style hit on his hands. Only 4.5 in. by 2.4 in. in size, the device reimagined the way cell phones work, most significantly through its revolutionary touch-sensitive interface, which streamlines key operations like text-messaging and makes resizing pictures a snap. Also enjoying a boom year were the folks at Nintendo, whose paradigm-shattering Wii video system, introduced for the holiday sales season in 2006, dominated the market in '07. Thanks to the system's motion-sensitive controller, geeks around the world rose to their feet, waved their arms and threw off the yoke of couch-potatodom, standing tall at last. ∎

Jobs' Style: The "i's" Have It

Steve Jobs' semiannual MacWorld product debuts are so predictable as to be the stuff of self-parody: Apple Computer's top man—always clad in black turtleneck, tennis shoes and jeans—reveals his latest gizmo; geeks swoon. Then again, Jobs, 52, is indeed an icon—he kick-started the personal computer revolution, back in the day—and the iPhone Apple released this year is an engineering marvel. When it went on sale in June, the few complaints it garnered involved the difficulties some experienced in activating the phone with Apple's telecommunications partner, AT&T, and the high price ($499) of the simplest iPhone. But Jobs ran into a buzzsaw on Sept. 5, when he declared Apple was immediately dropping the price by $200, aiming for the '07 holiday market. When owners howled, Apple offered a $100 in-store rebate to those who had paid full price for the iPhone before the cost was slashed.

Miyamoto's Magic: The "Wii's" Have It

In recent years, the Big Three of the video-game world—Nintendo, Microsoft and Sony—have focused on creating systems with ever more complex and dazzling graphics. It was time for a change, and the man who shifted the paradigm was the world's most admired creator of such fare, Nintendo's Shigeru Miyamoto, 54. The father of Mario, Donkey Kong, Zelda and other iconic digital entities shook up his field again in late 2006, when Nintendo released its Wii system, which sports an innovative controller that replicates a player's movements onscreen, as in the bowling game below. The Wii system, lo-res graphics and all, turned gaming from a passive to an active medium. Nintendo priced the new system at $250, hundreds of dollars below competing products. Result: in 2007 stores couldn't keep Wii systems on the shelves, and consumers fled to eBay to pay a premium for them.

Notebook

Immigration Reform Fails Again

Central American men, above, hop a Mexican freight train bound for the U.S., a trickle in the vast stream of illegal immigrants that continues to roil the U.S. social fabric. Yet once again in 2007, Congress could not reach consensus on how to solve the pressing problem. A Senate bill pushed by the White House and supported by a cross section of Republicans and Democrats would have required 20,000 new border agents, along with hundreds of miles of new fences and barriers, and a new worker verification system. Illegal aliens in the U.S. before 2007 would need to obtain a new Z visa, offering a path to citizenship that involved paying fines, passing medical and background checks, having a job, learning English, and (in many cases) returning to their home countries before applying. No go: critics branded the plan as granting amnesty to illegals, and the bill failed.

GERRY BROOME—POOL—AP IMAGES

All His Trials

In the dénouement of a case that pushed America's hot buttons on race, sports and privilege, Durham County, N.C., District Attorney Michael Nifong resigned his position and was disbarred in 2007. Nifong, 57, had charged several members of the Duke University lacrosse team with sexual assault in March 2006, after an exotic dancer claimed she had been raped at an off-campus house in which members of the team were partying. All charges in the case were dropped in April 2007, and in October three members of the lacrosse team filed a federal lawsuit against Nifong, the City of Durham and police detectives who investigated the allegations.

ANTHONY SUAU FOR TIME

KATHY WILLENS—AP IMAGES

Sales from the Crypt

In the latest controversy in biblical archaeology, Israeli producer Simcha Jacobovici and U.S. director James Cameron, left, teamed up on a book and Discovery Channel program claiming that 10 bone boxes from an ancient Jerusalem-area crypt bear such a suggestive roster of names (JESUS, SON OF JOSEPH, MARY) that it must be the holy family's tomb. They also argued that one inscription, MARIAMENE E MARA, denotes Mary Magdalene, and another, JUDAH SON OF JESUS, her son by the Saviour—thus challenging the Resurrection of Christ and positing a very holy union. The claims took a shelling from scholars. TIME's David Van Biema found the arguments "too dependent on stretched scholarship and conjecture" and cited a new publishing peril: "one-too-many-speculative-Bible-books syndrome."

A Rocky Road for Detroit

American automakers struggled throughout 2007, as bad tidings outweighed the good. After nine difficult years of attempting to unite two vastly different cultures, Daimler-Chrysler sold 81% of its ailing Chrysler division to a private equity fund, Cerberus Capital Management. Cerberus tapped Robert Nardelli, below, who left his post as CEO of Home Depot with a $210 million goodbye package, to run Chrysler, which lost $1.4 billion in 2006. Chrysler is now the No. 5 maker of cars in America, behind General Motors, Toyota, Ford Motor and Honda. Cerberus paid $7.4 billion for Chrysler, but

Daimler covered much of the cost.
General Motors and Chrysler both dodged a bullet in the fall, when they signed new four-year contracts with the United Auto-workers Union (UAW) after brief walkouts. In both cases, the union agreed to set up trust funds to pay future health benefits to workers. UAW negotiations with Ford, which lost $12.6 billion in 2006, were ongoing at press time.

Troubles in Toyland

In a long-running scandal that soiled some of the most famous names in American retailing—and such beloved children's toys as Barbie dolls and Thomas the Tank Engine train sets—U.S. toy companies were forced in 2007 to issue a series of recalls of playthings made in China. Most of the toys were recalled for containing high levels of harmful lead; the problems peaked in September, when giant toymaker Mattel was forced to recall more than 19 million items. The crisis roiled relations between the U.S. and China, which manufactures a whopping 80% of the world's toys. The Toy Industry Association, a U.S. trade group, announced a three-part plan that called for a federal requirement for mandatory safety-testing; industry-wide standards for such tests; and further certification by independent labs. Until the plan is adopted: caveat emptor.

As Home Prices Fall, Heads Roll on Wall Street

What's that giant popping sound? It's the noise of the U.S. housing-price bubble finally imploding, as homeowners around the country suffered steep declines in the value of their houses. After years of expansion, the correction was tough: house prices dropped 3.2% in the 12 months ending in June, banks foreclosed on low-cost subprime mortgages, and home sales dried up. When the Labor Department reported in September that job creation was stalling, worried economists began tossing about the R-word: recession. As the chain reaction continued, giant Wall Street firms were left holding the bag on billions in bad suprime mortgages and the stock market slumped badly. When quarterly reports showed huge losses, CEOs Stanley O'Neal of Merrill Lynch and Charles O. Prince of Citigroup were forced to resign—and many more were imperiled.

Islam Gets in the Swim

It wasn't even a contest: the clear winner of the closely watched competition for Portmanteau Word of the Year was the novel coinage burqini. The term was crafted by Lebanese-Australian Aheda Zanetti to describe the swimwear she created for Muslim women who seek to swim without violating Islam's dictates on female modesty. At right, the burqa-meets-bikini is modeled on Sydney's North Cronulla Beach by lifeguard Mecca Laa Laa. The suits became a hit, moving beyond the Muslim market to appeal to conservative Christians, cancer patients, burn victims and senior citizens.

Sport

Without a Net

France's Alain Robert, 45, makes a rope traverse high atop the ADIA skyscraper in Abu Dhabi, United Arab Emirates. Vertical daredevil Robert, who styles himself "Spider-Man," has climbed some of the world's tallest buildings—using only his hands. Among the heights he has scaled: the Eiffel Tower, the Sydney Opera House, the Sears Tower in Chicago and the world's tallest building, Taipei 101 in Taiwan. Robert was briefly detained by police in September 2007 after climbing the 795-ft. Federation Tower West office building in Moscow. His fame is growing in tandem with that of *parkour*, a French-born form of gutsy urban acrobatics. Robert later "summited" this building, sans ropes.

Joe Torre

"Say it ain't so, Joe!" A Yankee hero rides into the sunset

NO, YOUR EYES AREN'T DECEIVING YOU: THE GENT in Los Angeles Dodgers gear below is indeed the celebrated and beloved longtime manager of the New York Yankees, Joe Torre. On Nov. 1, Torre shucked off his Yankee pinstripes and donned Dodger blue after signing a three-year, $13 million deal that made him the new skipper of the recently hapless Dodgers. His trek thus echoed in miniature the famed 1958 exodus when the Dodgers left Ebbets Field in Brooklyn for the green pastures of L.A. Torre, who grew up in Brooklyn as a New York Giants fan, well recalls that historic migration.

Why would Torre, who is widely credited with restoring the luster to the Yankees, leave the single most famous team in sports? Simple: Yankees owner George Steinbrenner made him an offer he could refuse. "The Boss," as the crusty Steinbrenner is called in New York City tabloids, is now 77 and ailing, and his sons Hank and Hal are increasingly taking the helm of the team. None of the three were happy that their millionaire minions, under Torre's leadership, had failed to advance past the first round of the American League playoffs in each of the past three years. Never mind that Torre had taken the Yankees to the playoffs in every one of his 12 years with the team, and had won the World Series in four of his first five years. When the Yankees offered Torre a one-year contract that would

cut his pay unless the team won the Series, Torre, 67, took Horace Greeley's advice: Go west, old man.

For Torre, Los Angeles will be just another stop on the way to Cooperstown. After making his major-league debut with the Milwaukee Braves in 1960, he played for 17 years with the Braves, St. Louis Cardinals and New York Mets, was a nine-time All Star and retired with a lifetime batting average of .297. He's the winningest postseason manager in baseball history. In New York City, his decency and class made Steinbrenner's old "Bronx Zoo" a fading memory. And don't forget Torre's refreshing humor: when news choppers circled over his suburban home while he was being wooed by the Dodgers, he allowed, "The worst part about the helicopters is they showed I had a bald spot." ∎

Manny Ramirez
He reigns over Red Sox Nation

AFTER THE BOSTON RED SOX ROLLED OVER THE HAPLESS Colorado Rockies to win the 2007 World Series in a four-game sweep, headline after headline queried, ARE THE RED SOX THE NEW YANKEES? The thought would have been laughable not so long ago, for it was only in 2004 that the Bosox finally broke their fabled "curse" and won their first World Series in 86 years. But the 2007 Red Sox were so dominant that the comparison seemed apt. And if so, there was no question as to who was the new Babe Ruth: one reason fans everywhere were pulling for Boston to win the American League pennant was the chance to see Red Sox left-fielder Manny Ramirez compete again on the game's grandest stage

Ramirez, 35, is exactly what baseball needs more of these days: in his 15th season in the majors, the native of the Dominican Republic, who grew up in Yankee Country in New York City, is a shoo-in first-ballot Hall of Famer. More important, he's a gas, a larger-than-life character who is easily the game's most colorful player. In addition to his terrific stats—a lifetime batting average of .313, an All Star 11 times, 490 homers (and counting)— it's his unique style that makes fans smile just to catch a glimpse of him: the dreadlocks, the extra-long droopy pants, the big wide grin. And then there are the countless examples of "Manny being Manny": his weird disappearances into Fenway Park's famed Green Monster when pitchers are changed; his habit of losing his helmet as he runs the bases; his fabled lapses of concentration (O.K., those can be painful for the true Boston fans out there).

Truth to tell, 2007 wasn't Manny's best season; fighting a pulled muscle, he ended up with a .296 batting average. But maybe he was just biding his time. In the postseason, he batted .348, hit four home runs and drove in 16 runs. The bottom line? When Manny's in the house and his dreadlocks and helmet are flying, there's nothing but joy in Mudville. ■

Jeff Gordon

The man wins races, but can he ever win over the fans?

H E MAY BE USED TO NEGOTIATING TIGHT SPOTS, but Jeff Gordon, a dominant NASCAR driver for well over a decade, can't solve his ongoing predicament: often first on the racetrack, he is last in the hearts of the countrymen who are the sport's biggest fans. Humble and handsome, Gordon, 36, was racing quarter-midget cars at 5, sprint cars at 12 and stock cars shortly after he got his driver's license. When he was only 24, he won seven NASCAR races and the prestigious Winston Cup championship. Gordon had 10 wins each in 1996 and '97 and a modern era record-tying 13 in '98.

In 2007 Gordon drove in his 500th race, notched six wins, passed icon Dale Earnhardt's victory total and enjoyed a personal milestone when daughter Ella

Sofia Gordon was born in June. After an outstanding regular season, he was topped in the postseason Chase series by a driver he personally brought to his Hendrick Motorsports team, Jimmie Johnson. Gordon was generous with his praise for his friend.

So why don't more fans like him? Married to a supermodel, arriving at races in his private jet, Gordon may seem a tad too slick to the good-ole boys in the grandstand. Born in California, raised in Indiana and now living in New York City, he doesn't share stock-car racing's Southern-fried roots. Perhaps more important, Stars and Bars–wearing NASCAR fans think of themselves as ornery rebels at heart, and, as Gordon's business partner, Rick Hendrick, says, "Jeff ... is about as damn near perfect as you can get." ∎

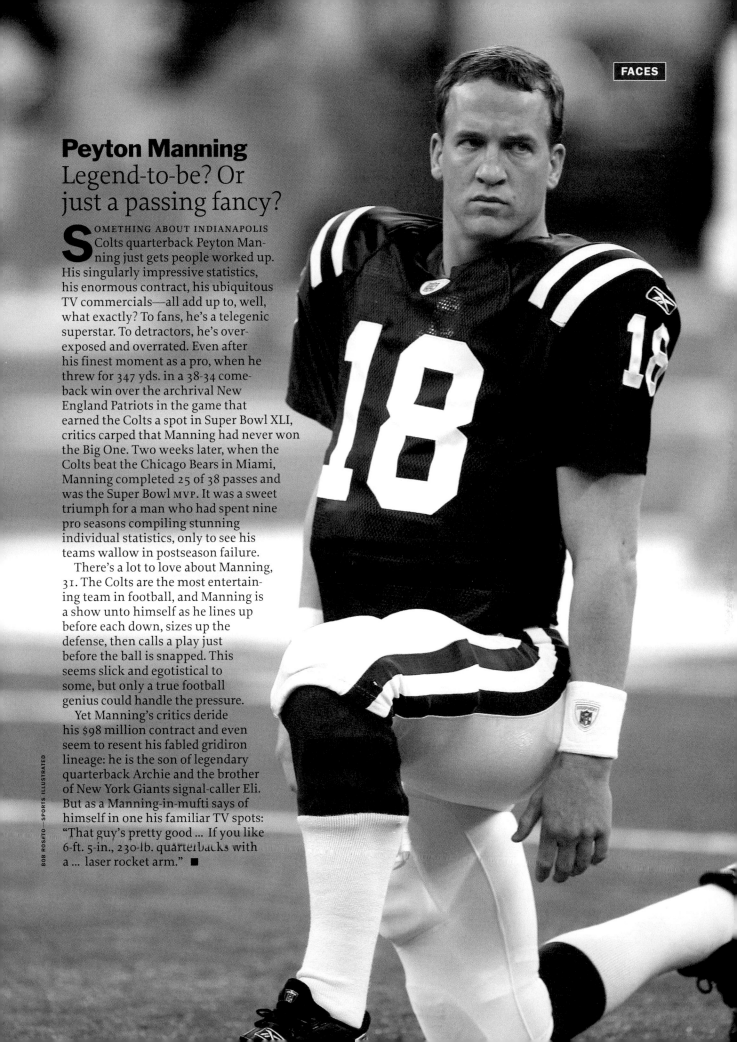

Peyton Manning
Legend-to-be? Or just a passing fancy?

SOMETHING ABOUT INDIANAPOLIS Colts quarterback Peyton Manning just gets people worked up. His singularly impressive statistics, his enormous contract, his ubiquitous TV commercials—all add up to, well, what exactly? To fans, he's a telegenic superstar. To detractors, he's overexposed and overrated. Even after his finest moment as a pro, when he threw for 347 yds. in a 38-34 comeback win over the archrival New England Patriots in the game that earned the Colts a spot in Super Bowl XLI, critics carped that Manning had never won the Big One. Two weeks later, when the Colts beat the Chicago Bears in Miami, Manning completed 25 of 38 passes and was the Super Bowl MVP. It was a sweet triumph for a man who had spent nine pro seasons compiling stunning individual statistics, only to see his teams wallow in postseason failure.

There's a lot to love about Manning, 31. The Colts are the most entertaining team in football, and Manning is a show unto himself as he lines up before each down, sizes up the defense, then calls a play just before the ball is snapped. This seems slick and egotistical to some, but only a true football genius could handle the pressure.

Yet Manning's critics deride his $98 million contract and even seem to resent his fabled gridiron lineage: he is the son of legendary quarterback Archie and the brother of New York Giants signal-caller Eli. But as a Manning-in-mufti says of himself in one his familiar TV spots: "That guy's pretty good ... If you like 6-ft. 5-in., 230-lb. quarterbacks with a ... laser rocket arm." ∎

Roger Federer

Like Tiger Woods, the cool Swiss dominates his sport, and for admiring duffers and hackers, there's a satisfying resonance in their growing friendship. But Federer, 26, has one thing Tiger doesn't: an Achilles' heel. In 2007 he racked up victories in three of the world's top four tournaments—winning the Australian and U.S. Opens and at Wimbledon—but he finished second, again, to Rafael Nadal on the clay courts of France. Until Federer wins at Roland Garros in Paris, his claim to being his game's greatest male player ever will be incomplete. At left, Federer studies a stroke at Wimbledon.

Living Legends

These are the good old days for Sunday spectators, as Tiger Woods and Roger Federer effortlessly continue to reign over their sports

Venus Williams

After a few shaky years, the sisters Williams are back on track. Serena, 26, won the Australian Open, and lanky Venus, 27, took her fourth Wimbledon title, left. But Venus lost in the semifinals of the U.S. Open to No. 1–ranked Justine Henin.

Rafael Nadal

Tennis lovers are pulling for the dashing Spaniard to become the challenging nemesis Federer (and the sport) deserves. But though he foiled Roger again in the French Open final, Nadal, still only 21, couldn't muster his mojo when his backdrop was green rather than orange.

STUART FRANKLIN—GETTY IMAGES

Tiger Woods

Woods was in a charitable mood this year; he won only one of golf's four major events, the PGA tourney in Tulsa, Okla., left, putting him at 13 in his pursuit of Jack Nicklaus' record of 18 major wins. At 31, he notched his 60th PGA tour victory at the BMW Championship. Although contending, Tiger couldn't mount a charge to win the U.S. Open, but he scored a victory the next day, when daughter Sam Alexis was born. Just to prove he's mortal, he underwent LASIK eye surgery in April.

Lorena Ochoa

The slim Mexican snatched the title of world's No. 1 from Annika Sörenstam in 2007, then iced her new status by winning the Women's British Open with a wire-to-wire victory at golf's home, the Old Course at St. Andrews. Ochoa, 26, won the next two LPGA tournaments for good measure.

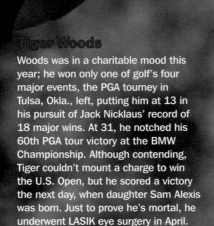

MATT DUNHAM—AP IMAGES

ELISE AMANDOLA—AP IMAGES

CHRIS MCGRATH—GETTY IMAGES

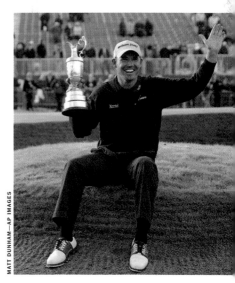

MATT DUNHAM—AP IMAGES

Zach Johnson

Johnson, 31, had won only two PGA championships before coming out of nowhere to win the Masters Tournament, fending off the celebrated trio of Tiger Woods, Retief Goosen and Rory Sabbatini to win the green jacket by two strokes. The famed Augusta, Ga., course proved a harsh test in 2007, and Johnson's winning score, 289, was a tie for the highest ever.

Angel Cabrera

The popular Argentine pro, 38, is called "the Duck." No Tiger, he's soft around the middle and at the edges, shunning a worried mien for a happy-go-lucky attitude. All golf cheered when Cabrera won the U.S. Open at Pennsylvania's Oakmont Country Club.

Padraig Harrington

At 36, the popular, improving star finally came out of his second-place rut and became the first Irishman to win the British Open in 60 years. Harrington beat Sergio Garcia in a thrilling four-hole playoff to win the Claret Jug.

Halls of Shame

Once again the year's sports pages resembled a crime blotter, as drug abuse tarnished medals and a quarterback went to the dogs

Barry Bonds

He is one of the greatest sluggers in history, but many fans believe Bonds, 43, used steroids in the past, as two respected journalists charged in the 2006 book *Game of Shadows.* After Bonds swatted homer No. 756, above, on Aug. 7, to pass Hank Aaron as the all-time home-run king, few beyond San Francisco cheered. On Nov. 15, Bonds was indicted on charges of perjury and obstruction of justice by a federal grand jury on grounds that he lied under oath about his alleged steroid use during an earlier inquiry.

Marion Jones

The popular track star, 32, who ran away with a harvest of five gold medals at the 2000 Olympic Games in Sydney, pleaded guilty on Oct. 5 to having lied about her use of steroids. Stripped of her Olympic medals, she said, "I have betrayed your trust ... I have let my country down, and I have let myself down."

BAS CZERWINSKI—AP IMAGES

Michael Vick

We've grown accustomed to stories of the abuse of steroids and other performance-enhancing substances in recent years. But no one could have predicted that one of the N.F.L.'s most promising young players would be involved in staging dogfights for "sport." On Aug. 24, the Atlanta Falcons' star quarterback, Michael Vick, 27, pleaded guilty to operating a dogfighting ring on his property in Virginia and to knowing that his partners in the operation killed dogs that didn't perform well. He is due to be sentenced in December 2007.

HARAZ N. GHANBARI—AP IMAGES

Tour de France

Going downhill—like these gents in the French Alps during Stage 9 of cycling's greatest event, the Tour de France—is easy. But cycling is facing a very tough uphill journey if it is to regain the respect of fans. In this year's race—wags dubbed it the Tour de Farce—several top stars were barred from competing before the start for doping violations, and leader Michael Rasmussen was sent home mid-race after being accused of lying about his pre-race training program. On Sept. 20, international arbitrators upheld the stripping of the 2006 title from American Floyd Landis for doping violations.

And in This Corner, the Good Guys

Fans looking for that rarest of commodities in today's sports world—heroes—rejoiced in the superlative play of the 2007 N.B.A. champs, the San Antonio Spurs. Led by power forward Tim Duncan, with trophy, and point guard Tony Parker (one of the rare U.S. hoop stars to hail from France), the Spurs cemented their claim to being one of the pro game's greatest-ever franchises when they swept the Cleveland Cavaliers in four games to win their third title in five years. The Spurs, like the unassuming and widely admired Duncan, 31, are models of consistency and low-key class. They make winning seem so natural that it's easy to forget how dominating they are in their sport.

The Cavaliers may not have proved a match for the Spurs, but at only 22, their leader, forward LeBron James, served notice that he may become one of the N.B.A.'s greatest stars, thrilling fans with his magnificent play against the Detroit Pistons in the Eastern Conference finals.

ERIC GAY—AP IMAGES

Notebook

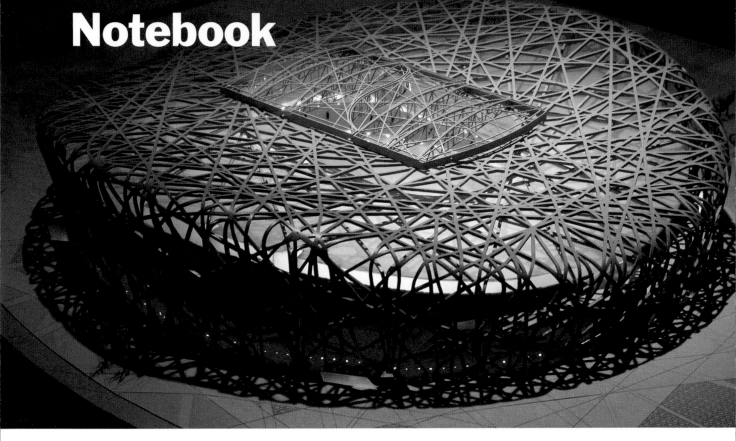

A Bird's Nest in Beijing

The Summer Games won't open in Beijing until Aug. 8, 2008, but the Chinese, determined to make the event a showcase for their rapidly changing nation, want to ensure the setting, if not the athletics, will be spectacular. Experts estimate Beijing's total Olympics-related expenditures will hit $38 billion, some four times as much as Greece spent preparing Athens for the 2004 Games. Eleven of the 12 sporting venues are on track to be finished by the end of 2007—and some of the structures, like the "Bird's Nest" main stadium, seen above in a rendering by architects Herzog & De Meuron, are dazzling. A new subway line to the airport will open a month before the opening ceremony, and a brand-new airport terminal designed by Norman Foster is slated to open in early 2008. Let the Games begin!

GEORGE WIDMAN—AP IMAGES

Farewell, Champion

He won the 2006 Kentucky Derby by 6-some lengths, going away, but only two weeks later, he shattered his right hind leg in the Preakness. Barbaro may have left the racetrack with his promise unfulfilled, but in his eight-month struggle to survive before his death in February, he became the most enriching story in sports, the warm center of a high-wire drama that featured two owners who spared no expense trying to save him; a team of caregivers at the University of Pennsylvania's New Bolton Center who nursed him through surgeries and bouts of deadly laminitis; and thousands of fans around the country who sent cards, flowers and prayers for his recovery.

ALESSANDRO DIGAETANA—POLARIS

SAURABH DAS—AP IMAGES

Brazil Dances Past the U.S. in the World Cup

Time seemed to be the foremost enemy of the U.S. women's soccer team in 2007. The athletes struggled with ghosts, trying to live up to the memory of Mia Hamm, Brandi Chastain and the other champions of the 1999 team. And in this year's World Cup, staged in China, even the clock seemed to work against the U.S.: the time difference meant that many games ran live on TV at 5 a.m. in the States. Even so, the U.S. women started strong: led by high-scoring Abby Wambach, left, at forward, the team went undefeated to win their division, then beat England 3-0 in the quarterfinals. But in the semifinals, Brazil's "samba queens" schooled the Americans—diverted by coach Greg Ryan's decision to insert veteran goalie Brianna Scurry over starter Hope Solo—whipping them 4-0. The Americans consoled themselves by beating Norway 4-1 to earn third place.

Football's Perfect Toss: Brady to Moss

Restless athletes have a standard gripe: "If I could just play with the right team, I'd show you what I can do." The argument gets old, but in the case of the gifted wide receiver Randy Moss, it certainly rang true in 2007. It didn't hurt that when Moss, 30, finally found the right team, it just happened to be one of the great dynasties in recent N.F.L. history: the New England Patriots. The Pats were already strong without Moss, but after the man who seemed to sulk through his final seasons with the Minnesota Vikings and Oakland Raiders hooked up with quarterback Tom Brady, opposing defenses were simply outclassed. In his first 10 games as a Patriot, Moss scored 16 touchdowns and ended up on the cover of SPORTS ILLUSTRATED. Meanwhile, a similar story was playing out in Dallas, where receiver Terrell Owens played brilliantly in his second year with the rejuvenated Cowboys.

DAVID DUPREY—AP IMAGES

Sails Meeting

Crew members scramble up the masts of the two sloops, left, that competed for sailing's most prized trophy, the America's Cup, in June and July. Team New Zealand's *NZL-92* is on the right; Swiss Alinghi's *SUI-100* is at left.

Ironically, few Americans tuned into the event that bears their hemisphere's name; sailing is one of those sports that appeal to Yankees only when Yankees are at the helm. And that's too bad: raced off the coast of Valencia, Spain, the 32nd Cup will be remembered as one of history's finest. The Swiss won 5-2, which might not suggest that the best-of-nine series was all that close. But indeed it was, at a time when the contest for the oldest trophy in sport was crying out for a ding-dong battle.

In Valencia the average winning margin was 24 sec.—about half a dozen boat lengths. After whitewashes at the previous three Cups, here was a series to savor. The Kiwis stunned the defending Swiss team by winning two of the first three races. The remaining battles were fierce and peppered with lead changes, but a slightly better Alinghi crew proved decisive, perhaps because they had five Kiwis in their 17-man crew. Oh, yes: Switzerland is indeed landlocked. Just another reason to love the Cup.

BERNAT ARMANGUE—AP IMAGES

Science

War of the Worlds—Not

Scientists working at the Very Large Telescope (VLT) site atop 8,645-ft. Cerro Paranai in Chile direct a powerful laser beam at the center of the Milky Way galaxy. The laser beam thrust, however martial in appearance, is designed to facilitate imaging of faraway objects. Atoms are excited by the beam, allowing the astronomers to measure the extent of the distortion of vision that is created by Earth's atmosphere. The readings are then fed into the VLT's computers, which modify the curvature of the observatory's four optical telescopes to compensate for the distortion. Observers who might happen to be looking back at Earth—assuming there are any—would see the laser beam combining with light from our sun to form a single dot of light about as bright as one of the myriad stars visible in this night skyscape.

Richard Branson
Wings of desire

CALL RICHARD BRANSON THE 57-YEAR-OLD VIRGIN. And not because the British tycoon has transformed the V-word into one of the world's most recognized brands by pasting it on everything from airlines, mobile phones and music stores to comic books and cola. Rather, because he comes to each new venture with the fresh, unjaded enthusiasm of a man building a business for the first time. No venture has excited him more, though, than Virgin Galactic, which plans to launch a space tourism industry (at $200,000 for a two-hour flight; more than 175 tickets have already been sold) by 2009. A Virgin Galactic vehicle prototype is taking shape on a hangar floor in California's Mojave Desert, and Branson is so sure it will fly that he plans to take his two kids, his 91-year-old dad and his 88-year-old mom on the first flight.

The year 2007, though, was one of both transition and tragedy for Branson. In July, rocket fuel exploded at the California plant where the Virgin Galactic spacecraft was being assembled, killing three people. In September his close friend, aviator Steve Fossett (many of whose adventures Branson had financed), disappeared while flying over the Nevada desert; he has not been found, and is believed to have perished.

Always a visionary, Branson has become fascinated by science and the global environment; now he is using his wealth and his flair for nutty promotional stunts to stimulate research. In February he set up a $25 million prize for the first scientist who comes up with a system for extracting greenhouse gases from the atmosphere, and he spent much of '07 hawking his latest project: Virgin Fuels, which hopes to market a clean, affordable alternative to gasoline in the near future. Make that synthetic oil extra-Virgin, please? ∎

Pharaoh Hatshepsut
After 17 centuries of denial on the Nile, she's back!

ER NAME MEANS "THE FIRST RESPECTABLE LADY," and Hatshepsut may finally be getting the respect she deserves. The only woman in ancient Egypt to assume the title of Pharaoh (both Cleopatra and Nefertiti were denied this honor), she ruled during the 15th century B.C., often dressing like a man and wearing a false beard fashioned from wood. But she was succeeded by a stepson who despised her and tried to erase from the historical record all traces of her reign. Archaeologists believe this explains why her mummy vanished shortly after her death, leaving scholars to puzzle about details of her rule over the New Kingdom, which saw the last great flowering of pharaonic power.

But in June, a tooth retrieved from a wooden box known to be associated with Hatshepsut (it contained the female Pharaoh's embalmed organs) was discovered to fit perfectly into the jaw of a previously unidentified woman, unearthed separately, whose mummified remains date from the same era and were found in 1903. Later DNA tests confirmed that this anonymous mummy's genetic material was a close match to samples taken from bodies known to belong to the Egyptian royal family. All of which makes Hatshepsut's mummy the first of any Egyptian ruler to be found and positively identified since King Tut's tomb was opened in 1922. Seems some mummies just won't keep mum. ∎

Forecast: Changeable

As awareness of the threat posed by global warming grows, disasters caused by weather take on added significance

MOTHER NATURE'S SCOURING PADS—DUST STORMS, floods and wildfires—play an essential role in the planet's cycle of growth and decay. But as scientists, leaders and individuals around the world awaken to the perils created by the gradual warming of the globe, every weather-related calamity is examined for its relationship to Earth's changing climate, even though scientists caution that it is difficult to make direct connections between specific, localized events and climatic patterns operating across vast expanses of time and space. Even so, Britain's Prime Minister Gordon Brown voiced the concerns of many when he said, after flying over villages in central England swamped by the heaviest flooding in six decades, "Like every advanced industrialized country, we are coming to terms with the issues surrounding climate change."

Indeed, though scientists predict that warming temperatures in tropical waters will breed ever larger and more destructive tropical storms, the 2007 U.S. hurricane season passed uneventfully. But such welcome news should not be construed as evidence that global warming is overhyped. As a February 2007 report from the U.N.'s Intergovernmental Panel on Climate Change declared, "Warming of the climate system is unequivocal." The report also concluded, "with very high confidence," that human activities since 1750 have played a major role in the process, as greenhouse gases help trap solar heat that would otherwise radiate away. ■

KEVORK DJANSEZIAN—AP IMAGES

Floods in India

Above, a young boy paddles through his submerged village near Guwahati, in India's eastern state of Assam, in July. Monsoon rains were very heavy in 2007; they are critical to the natural calendar of the subcontinent, and scientists fear that such well-established weather patterns may be disrupted by global warming.

Wildfires on Catalina Island

Wildfires are common—and an essential part of the natural cycle—in Southern California and across the U.S. West, but such fires have become larger and more frequent in recent years. Some firefighters who battled this blaze on the idyllic resort island of Catalina in May arrived after mopping up a major fire that raged in Los Angeles' sprawling Griffith Park.

A Haboob in Sudan

A gigantic haboob, or sand storm, rolls into Khartoum, the capital of Sudan, on April 29. Haboobs are found where sand and wind are plentiful but soil is scarce—conditions common in many areas of Africa, as well as in the U.S. Southwest. Similar storms, with dust replacing sand, ravaged the American Midwest during the Dust Bowl days of the 1930s. Scientists have now learned that some minerals found in the rain forests of South America were carried into the atmosphere by haboobs, then borne across the ocean by jet streams—a reminder of the complexity and enormity of Earth's ecosystem.

Floods in the U.S. Midwest

When an unusually heavy rainy spell in late summer spawned flash floods across the Midwest, the home above in Stockton, Minn., was ripped from its foundations on Aug. 20 and came to rest on nearby railroad tracks. As floodwaters rose, seven people were killed in southeastern Minnesota and hundreds of homes were destroyed over a three-country area. Homeland Security Secretary Michael Chertoff visited the scene, arriving directly from Ohio, which was also hard-hit by floods. On Aug 23 President George W. Bush declared the Minnesota region a federal disaster area.

Floods in Central England

Villages, fields and hedgerows in central England were swallowed up by floodwaters after heavy rains sent rivers and creeks swelling over their banks in midsummer. At left, the historic village of Tewkesbury in Gloucestershire seems to have retreated behind a brown moat formed by the waters of the River Severn on July 22. The floods, the most severe to strike the region in 60 years, left hundreds of thousands of Britons without drinking water and power.

Kicking Habits

Exploring the brain to find out how addiction affects our bodies, scientists are opening the door to potential cures

THE BAD NEWS: ADDICTION TO HARMFUL SUBSTANCES and behaviors continues to be a major problem in the U.S. The good news: over the past 10 years, researchers have made real progress in understanding the physical basis of addiction. Armed with increasingly sophisticated technologies, including fMRIS and PET scans, investigators have begun to figure out exactly what goes wrong in the brain of an addict—which neurotransmitting chemicals are out of balance and what regions of the brain are affected. They are developing a more detailed understanding of how deeply and completely addiction can affect the brain, by hijacking memory-making processes and by exploiting emotions. And that's helped them design new drug treatments that are showing promise in cutting off the craving that drives an addict irresistibly toward relapse, a risk facing even the most dedicated abstainer.

Researchers exploring the brain's reward system, powered largely by the neurotransmitter dopamine, are focusing on the family of dopamine receptors that populate nerve cells and bind to the compound. The hope is that if you can dampen the effect of the brain chemical that carries the pleasurable signal, you can loosen the drug's hold. For example, one particular group of dopamine receptors, called D3, seems to multiply in the presence of cocaine, methamphetamine and nicotine, making it possible for more of the drug to enter and activate nerve cells.

If dopamine receptors are the gas, the brain's own inhibitory systems act as the brakes. But in addicts, this natural damping circuit, called GABA (gamma-aminobutyric acid), appears to be faulty, so the brain never appreciates that it has been satiated.

Enter vigabatrin, an antiepilepsy drug marketed in 60 countries (but not yet in the U.S.). An effective GABA booster, vigabatrin helps epileptics suppress the overactive motor neurons that can cause muscles to go into spasm. Suspecting that enhancing the GABA levels in addicts' brains might help them control their drug cravings, two U.S. biotech firms are studying vigabatrin's effect on methamphetamine and cocaine users. So far, in animals, vigabatrin prevents the breakdown of GABA so that more of the inhibitory compound can be stored in whole form in nerve cells. That way, more of it could be released when those cells are activated by a hit from a drug. Researchers hope vigabatrin may be effective against all forms of addiction.

Another important discovery: evidence is building to support the 90-day rehabilitation model, which is used by Alcoholics Anonymous (new AA members are urged to attend daily meetings for their first 90 days) and is the length of most stints in drug-treatment programs. It turns out that this is just about how long it takes for the brain to reset itself and shake off the immediate influence of a drug. Researchers at Yale University have documented what they call the sleeper effect—a gradual re-engaging of proper decision making and analytical functions in the brain's prefrontal cortex—after an addict has abstained for at least 90 days.

This work has led to research on cognitive enhancers, or compounds that may amplify connections in the prefrontal cortex to speed up the natural reversal. Such enhancement would give the higher regions of the brain a fighting chance against the amygdala, a more basal region that plays a role in priming the dopamine-reward system when certain cues suggest imminent pleasure—anything from the sight of white powder that looks like cocaine to spending time with friends you used to drink with. It's that conditioned reflex that unleashes a craving.

More and more, scientists say that extinguishing urges is not simply a matter of getting one's cravings for substances or behavior to fade but of helping the addict learn a new form of conditioning, a sort of rewiring that allows the brain's cognitive power to shout down the amygdala and other lower regions. Or, as recovering alcoholics say in AA: "Recovery is a process, not an event; it takes time." ∎

Alcohol About **18.7 million** people, or 7.7% of the population, are addicted to or abuse alcohol. Alcoholics Anonymous currently numbers only 2 million members.

CRYSTAL CARTIER PHOTOGRAPHY—CORBIS

Substance and Behavioral Addictions

Addicted America

Drugs An estimated **3.6 million** people are dependent on drugs. Each day some 8,000 people try them for the first time; 700,000 more are being treated for addiction. Cocaine, marijuana and prescription pain relievers are the most abused.

Tobacco There are about **71.5 million** users of tobacco products in the U.S. Some **23.4%** of men and **18.5%** of women are cigarette smokers, with cigarette use lowest in Western states and highest in the Midwest; 44.3% of young adults ages 18 to 25 use tobacco, the highest rate for any age group.

Caffeine It's the most widely used mood-altering drug in the world and is routinely ingested by about **80% to 90%** of Americans, primarily through soda and coffee. A daily brewed cup of joe, with 100 mg of caffeine, can lead to physical dependence. Withdrawal symptoms are experienced by **40% to 70%** of those trying to stop.

Sex About **16 million** Americans suffer from compulsive sexual behavior. A third are women; some **60%** of all sex addicts were abused in childhood. An addict is dependent on the neurochemical changes that take place during sex and is consumed by sexual thoughts. Other major U.S. addictions: gambling, food, shopping and the Internet.

What happens in the brain

1. We feel good when neurons in the reward pathway release a neurotransmitter called dopamine into the nucleus accumbens and other brain areas.

2. Neurons in the reward pathway communicate by sending electrical signals down their axons. The signal is passed to the next neuron across a small gap called the synapse.

3. Dopamine is released into the synapse, crosses to the next neuron and binds to receptors, providing a jolt of pleasure. Excess dopamine is taken back up by the sending cell. Other nerve cells release GABA, an inhibitory neurotransmitter that works to prevent the receptor nerve from being overstimulated.

4. Addictive substances increase the amount of dopamine in the synapse, heightening the feeling of pleasure. Addiction occurs when repeated drug use disrupts the normal balance of brain circuits that control rewards, memory and cognition, ultimately leading to compulsive drug taking.

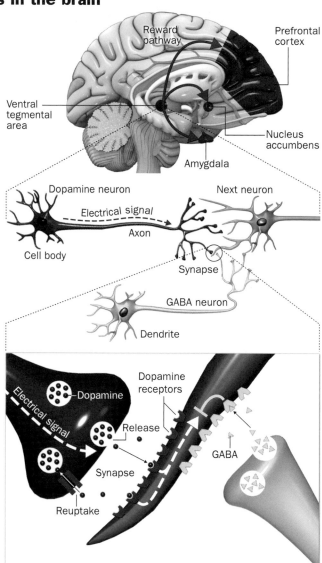

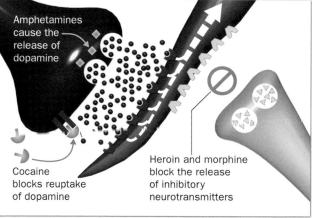

Source: National Institute on Drug Abuse (NIH)
TIME Diagram by Kristina Dell, Meg Massey and Joe Lertola

Notebook

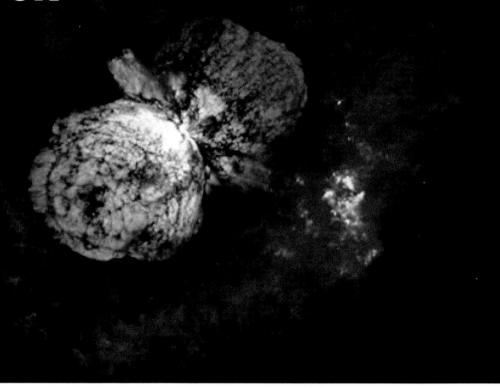

The Greatest Show in the Milky Way?

There's trouble in the neighborhood—well, assuming your definition of the 'hood includes the gorgeous star star Eta Carinae, above, which TIME science writer Jeffrey Kluger identified as "just 7,500 light-years away … square in our cosmic ZIP code." Astronomers are keeping an eye on Eta Carinae because its brightness has been fluctuating for two centuries, and lately it looks much the way the star known as SN 2006gy used to—before that star blew up in an explosion, recorded in 2007, that dwarfed the size of most supernovas, long the yardstick for massive cosmic blasts. The death of SN 2006gy was 100 times more powerful than that of a typical supernova; one astronomer called it "truly monstrous." Scientists say that if Eta Carinae does explode, we'll enjoy a terrific light show in the heavens, but Earth will be safe. Stand down, Al Gore.

Spaced Out, Big Time

Yes, the late Alan Shepard once made earthbound duffers laugh by hitting golf balls on the moon. But in 2007 Lisa Nowak upped the ante for astronaut antics. The veteran of one shuttle flight, 44, was arrested on Feb. 5 in Orlando, Fla., and charged with attempted kidnapping. The married mother of three allegedly drove from Houston to Orlando—packing a wig, pepper spray, a folding knife and rubber tubing—in hopes of kidnapping U.S. Air Force Captain Colleen Shipman, the girlfriend of William Oefelein, a divorced astronaut with whom Nowak also was romantically involved.

I Love Coffee, I Love Tea …

BZZZTTTT! If you're one of the people who needs a jolt of caffeine to get your motor running, you're in luck. With anywhere from 55% to 90% of the U.S population consuming caffeine every day (depending on which study you consult), the stuff is now turning up everywhere. Red Bull energy drink has the highest profile of the new caffeine-spiked products, but at every turn there are others: caffeine-infused gum, lip balm, mints, beer, candy, sunflower seeds, even soap—which claims to impart a boost through the skin. Sales of such supplements increased more than 55% in 2006 alone. TIME health guru Sanjay Gupta, M.D., says the products can't hurt but suggests moderation is in order.

Raptor of the Year

What's 26 ft. long, 16 ft. tall, weighs 3,000 lbs., hails from China and has feathered wings? No, it's not Houston Rockets center Yao Ming; he is, to quote Woody Allen's take on Emily Dickinson, "the thing without feathers." The thing *with* feathers is a new species of dinosaur found in the Erlian Basin of Inner Mongolia. Dubbed *Gigantoraptor erlianensis,* the big guy was about the size of a *T. rex.* But he threw a crimp in the theory that dinosaurs got smaller as they evolved into birds and that bigger dinosaurs had less birdlike characteristics: most of Giganto's fellow oviraptors are human-sized or smaller.

To Bee or Not to Bee?

In late 2006, entire hives of honeybees began dying overnight, victims of an unknown syndrome dubbed colony-collapse disorder (CCD). The die-offs have afflicted nearly half of U.S. beekeeping operations to date, and if you think this is a tempest in a honey-pot, think again: in the U.S., bees pollinate foods that add up to a harvest of some $15 billion. Scientists are currently investigating three theories about the agent that's causing CCD:
1. The culprit is a pathogen, Israeli acute paralysis virus, that is present in some 90% of the samples.
2. No, it's a tiny mite, the vampiric *Varroa destructor,* which sucks the blood of bees; it first appeared in the U.S. in 1987.
3. The CCD agent is pesticides, especially Imidacloprid, an ingredient marketed by Bayer and banned in France since 1999.

A Home Away from Home

At right, on June 13 astronaut Steven Swanson installs new solar arrays that provide power to the International Space Station. The station was a busy place in 2007. On Oct. 12, American Peggy Whitson, 47, became the first woman to serve as commander of the outpost. She faced a crisis only weeks later, when an old solar array tore while it was being redeployed. U.S. astronauts Scott Parazynski and Douglas Wheelock conducted an improvised emergency spacewalk and fixed the problem. On Nov. 24, Whitson and Daniel Tani connected the new Italian-built Harmony laboratory module to the station.

Arts

Arcs of Triumph

A miniaturist he's not. American sculptor Richard Serra, 68, works with enormous steel plates to create massive, sinuously curving configurations of space that can weigh more than a jetliner. When New York City's Museum of Modern Art mounted a Serra retrospective in the summer, assembling the works required two trailer trucks, a crane, a 40-.ft.-wide rolling gantry and a team of welders. The museum's new galleries, completed in 2004, were ready: they were designed to hold the enormous weight of Serra's pieces by curators anticipating the show. Hailing the exhibit, TIME critic Richard Lacayo said, "Serra, whose work had once seemed as severe and forbidding as any the 20th century had produced, had developed, indisputably, into one of the greatest living American artists ... and one of the most popular. You enter [his works] as you would a temple and absorb them by moving through them."

Justin Timberlake

Young smoothie

FOR SONG-AND-DANCE man Timberlake, 2007 was a very good year. His Future-Sex tour sold out in venues around the world, boosting *Summer Love*, the fourth single from his 2006 album *Future-Sex/LoveSounds*, into the Top 10. If the heartthrob was worried that his street cred might suffer from hosting the Nickelodeon Kids' Choice Awards, he needn't have been: three people were wounded by gunfire at an afterparty. Timberlake also voiced the part of a feckless royal heir in the animated hit *Shrek the Third*.

On the awards circuit, the one-time 'N Sync member, 26, beat out Bono, Beyoncé, Jay-Z and Kanye West for a "Quadruple Threat" award at the MTV Video Music Awards for his toils as singer, actor, restaurateur and impresario of a successful personal clothing line. His work on a *Saturday Night Live* musical sketch about an unusual holiday gift, *D___ in a Box*, earned him an Emmy for Outstanding Original Music and Lyrics while the video became a viral hit on YouTube. But no matter how many smooth moves Justin is bustin', there seems to be one stigma this rake just can't shake: his onetime courtship of Britney Spears. Get over it, America. ∎

Don Imus

Loose lips finally sink the ship of radio's longtime shock jock

SAY THIS FOR DON IMUS: THE MAN CAN TURN AN ECONOMICAL phrase. When the veteran radio ranter described the Rutgers women's basketball team as "nappy-headed hos" on the April 4 *Imus in the Morning* show, he packed so many layers of offense into the statement that it was a perfect little diamond of insult. There was a racial element, a gender element and even a class element, as he implied that the Scarlet Knights were thuggish and ghetto compared with the good-ole-gals of Tennessee's Lady Vols.

Imus, 67, was a famous, rich, old white man picking on a bunch of young, mostly black college women. So it seemed pretty cut-and-dried that his bosses at CBS Radio would slap his wrist, suspending his popular show—half frat party, half political salon for the Beltway élite—for two weeks, and that MSNBC would cancel the TV simulcast. And that Imus would meet with the students he offended. Case closed, justice served, lesson—possibly—learned. Move on.

Not this time. The firestorm only heated up as the days ticked by. Imus' repeated apologies—and boasts of his own decency, including his charity work, his support of black Senate candidate Harold Ford Jr., even his booking the black singing group Blind Boys of Alabama on his show—failed to silence the growing chorus of voices saying he must go. On April 12, CBS dropped the show. Early in December, a chastened Imus returned to a much smaller outlet, New York City station WABC—with two new black cast members in tow. ■

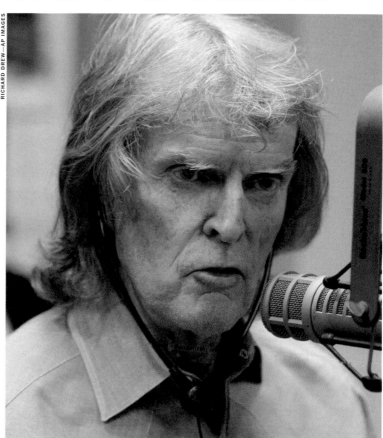

Judd Apatow
This just in: man writes funny movie about real people

BY RIGHTS, JUDD APATOW SHOULD BE A TERRIBLE filmmaker. The movies he writes and directs largely feature his friends and family, which is usually an invitation to lazy inside-joking. His subjects tend to be none-too-bright slackers and losers, which always carries the possibility of tiresome indulgence: O.K., they're kinda dumb, but isn't there something adorable in their stupidity? Yet Apatow represents, for the moment at least, the best in American movie comedy. *The 40 Year-Old Virgin* (2005) somehow made rather touching and funny sense out of that eponymous condition and its protagonist's recovery from it. The 2007 surprise summer smash *Knocked Up* did much the same thing for a much more common situation—the inconvenient consequences of a one-night stand. More important, it did so through characters who actually seemed real, and who made us care about them. Imagine that!

Apatow, 40, makes films that resonate with young audiences. But unlike the Hollywood teams that fash-ion comedies for the lowest common denominator, he is a real writer—one with something on his mind besides barf jokes and public flatulence (though he is not above such fare). He knows how to write funny, "he said, she said" jokes. More important, he's a ten-der observer of ordinary life. At heart, he's a square: a man who believes in marriage, family and bourgeois dutifulness, a throwback to the screenwriters who created the classic romantic comedies of the 1930s.

Most of today's movie comedies can be summed up in their pitch line: Jackie Chan meets Chris Tucker (again); hilarity ensues. They boast all the staying power of the popcorn boxes that accompany them. But Apatow's films get viewers engaged, thinking and arguing—like TIME's critics Richard Schickel and Richard Corliss, who disagreed so strongly over the merits of *Knocked Up* that they wrote long, strongly differing reviews of it for the magazine. Said Shickel: it is "a small and welcome miracle." Said Corliss: "It isn't that good." Discuss amongst yourselves. ∎

Shia LaBeouf
The kid gets the picture

SHIA WHO? YES, HE MAY BE A FRESH FACE, but as the human star of 2007's warring-alien-robot event film, *Transformers;* as the voice of the lead penguin in the animated *Surf's Up;* as the vulnerable bad boy in an '07 surprise hit, the Hitchcockian teen thriller *Disturbia;* and as Steven Spielberg's hand-picked choice to co-star with Harrison Ford and Cate Blanchett in the long-awaited fourth *Indiana Jones* movie, due in May 2008, LaBeouf is blowing up faster than a stunt car on a Michael Bay set.

LaBeouf, 21, is that rarest of modern screen creatures, the scrappy kid next door. With his giant brown eyes, lanky frame and indiscernible ethnicity (he's Jewish), he is a relatable foil for shiny robots and iconic heroes. His authenticity is hard-earned; he grew up in Los Angeles' Echo Park, a mainly Latino working-class neighborhood, the only child of a drug-addicted Vietnam-vet father and a hippie ballerina mother with a bum knee.

Envious of a fellow student whose acting gig bought him cool shoes, LaBeouf began working on a stand-up comedy act at only 10; his comic timing and impish little-brother face quickly got him TV work. By the time he was 14, he had acquired a cadre of kid fans and an Emmy as a lead on the Disney Channel show *Even Stevens.* At 16, LaBeouf moved into his own place in Burbank. Now he's coming into his own in a far larger arena: the screen of America's multiplexes. ■

Light Waves

Architect Steven Holl transforms a Kansas City museum's grand sloping lawn into a luminous waterfall of galleries

THE NELSON-ATKINS MUSEUM OF ART IN KANSAS City, Mo., is a serene neoclassical building from 1933. A stately terraced lawn with a sculpture garden pours down from the grand south entrance. Nine years ago, when the museum's director, Marc Wilson, and his trustees decided it was time to expand, they began a search for architects. Eventually they whittled the list down to six. Nearly all the finalists proposed building on the parking lot at the building's rear, a location that wouldn't interfere with its grand façade. Only Steven Holl dared to suggest an addition that would cascade down the eastern edge of the great lawn. Not only that, the expansion would actually be a series of pavilions, translucent glass enclosures over gallery spaces located mostly underground. He called them lenses. Most of them would be oddly shaped, and at night they would glow from within, like nests of light.

This may not sound like an idea that would go over well in down-to-earth Kansas City, but the local opposition, what there was of it, folded long ago. Beauty is an argument that doesn't take no for an answer. And when you're confronted with something as haunting and luminous as the Bloch Building, as the new addition is now called, what other word will do?

At twilight, when their interior lights come on, the lenses have a milky refulgence, radiating gently against the sky. In daylight, when the glass loses that ectoplasmic glow, there are a few dead zones along the exterior, stretches that have the featureless feel of shed walls. But to keep the eye occupied, Holl plays with the forms and arrangement of the five lenses, bending and dipping them as the hilly site also bends and dips. As you stroll down the slope, the building unfolds in surprising episodes. There's nothing quite like it anywhere else in the U.S.

Something old, something new
At left, the classical main building, with an oversized Claes Oldenburg shuttle-cock in front; at right, Holl's addition

Descending *The galleries tumble down-hill from the museum's main building*

What Holl has produced, working with his senior partner, Chris McVoy, is something that doesn't merely mimic the classicism of the older museum building but reformulates it in 21st century terms. As Holl puts it, he promised Wilson and the museum's trustees that "the new will be as new as can be, but the old will be preserved." If anything, he amplified the classicism of the space behind the old building by positioning the topmost, longest and most conventionally rectangular of his lenses at a perpendicular to the museum's rear façade. That created a square courtyard with a serene reflecting pool where the parking lot used to be.

Once you get inside, classical references are out, plunging diagonals are in. And though the gallery spaces are intricately conceived, they don't compete with the art, a complaint that's been raised against Frank Gehry's Guggenheim Museum Bilbao and Daniel Libeskind's addition to the Denver Art Museum. "I wanted a building that artists would appreciate," says Holl. So at eye level the galleries maintain their composure. It's overhead where he gets busier,

playing with tilted ceilings and oversize curving alcoves that operate like cloud formations—meaning there's always something interesting going on up there, but gently enough that it doesn't demand your full attention.

Holl has long simmered on the edge of superstardom. Until now, he was best known for a handful of highly regarded projects: a superb little church in Seattle, a much talked-about museum in Helsinki. But his tough-minded aesthetic positions have sometimes worked against him. So the Bloch Building is not just a triumph; it's a timely one. Those five glowing lenses are the kind of thing that can put your career in a whole new light. ■

"Author! Author!" *Rowling reads excerpts to spellbound fans in Lond*

No spoilers, please! *Clearly, suspense was building before the book's release*

Phoenix Daniel Radcliffe, left, returned as Harry in the fifth film

Exit Strategies: One

All's well that ends well: J.K. Rowling keeps her promise with a satisfying finale to the seven-volume saga of **Harry Potter**

WE ALL KNOW THE DRILL BY NOW: WHEN A NEW Harry Potter book goes on sale, fans around the world dutifully don wizard's hats, paint scars on their foreheads and haunt bookstores at midnight, eager to snatch up J.K. Rowling's latest installment in the genre she pioneered, the wizardly bildungsroman. Determined to foil plot spoilers, the publisher trots out ever more photogenic guarantees of the volume's virginity—the 2007 photo-op featured a lucite case to guard the treasured text. But this time around, when *Harry Potter and the Deathly Hallows* went on sale at the witching hour on July 21, the elation was touched with sadness, for this was the seventh volume in the series, and Rowling had declared long ago that Potter's story would end with this book.

In a sense, two stories ended that night. Potter and the good guys of the Order of the Phoenix ended their long struggle against uber-villain Lord Voldemort and his Death Eaters in satisfying fashion, with the loss of a few beloved characters and an Armageddon of a wind-up at the Hogwarts academy. But the second story was just as fascinating, for with the book's publication a surprising episode in modern cultural history also ended. Blockbuster movies and TV shows come and go, and there's a new smash video on YouTube every week. But in today's dwindling market for fiction, Rowling's Potter series stands out as a literary sensation without equal in decades. Finding a match for it might lead one back to the beginning of the 20th century, when Arthur Conan Doyle's Sherlock Holmes character was so beloved that after Conan Doyle tried to kill him off, he was forced by popular demand to revive him—an order of the phoenix if there ever was one.

The final *Potter* book, to no one's surprise, was the biggest-selling novel of 2007. For Rowling, it was icing on the cake: a few weeks earlier, the fifth film based on the series, *Harry Potter and the Order of the Phoenix,* took in $140 million at the U.S. box office in only five days. In short, Rowling and Potter ruled the summer of '07. Farewell, Harry! And thanks for the mummeries. ■

In media res James Gandolfini as Tony Soprano, Edie Falco as Carmella Soprano and Robert Iler as son A.J. take their final bow

Bang, One Whimper

All's well that ends … well, with a black screen and the major characters in limbo. Exeunt **The Sopranos,** tough-guy style

Y OU COULD ORGANIZE THE HISTORY OF TV DRAMAS into B.T. and A.T.: Before Tony and After Tony," Time TV critic James Poniewozick argued a few weeks after the final episode of the long-running hit series transfixed the nation. "Before *The Sopranos*," he said, "TV drama was mainly divided between good guys and bad guys (with the odd exception like *NYPD Blue's* Andy Sipowicz). Tony Soprano and his followers on HBO, FX and elsewhere showed that audiences would follow villains with sympathetic qualities and heroes with addictive, self-destructive personalities. Move over, good guys and bad guys, these dramas said. Make room for the good-bad guy."

Later in the summer, Poniewozick included *The Sopranos* on a Time list of 17 Shows That Changed TV. Indeed, writer David Chase's saga of New Jersey Mafia types dreaming of reviving the glory days of organized crime had long ago been anointed as one of the greatest series in the history of the medium, hailed for its unflinching realism, its moral ambiguity, its complex,

believable characters and its sympathetic exploration of Italian-American life. So when HBO announced that the series, which debuted in 1999, would end on June 10, fans went into a tizzy. Would the show end with a *Hamlet*-style slaughter of the main characters? Would Tony get "whacked"? Speculation abounded, but Chase surprised fans by ending the series in ambiguous fashion, picturing Tony, his wife and son having an ordinary meal in a diner, then going to a long, black screen. Result: howling fans, robbed of the consummation they so devoutly wished for, filled HBO's website with so many furious commentaries that it crashed.

But Poniewozick applauded, writing on his Time blog: "This is life and *The Sopranos*' view of it: no dramatic final poppings, no big finishes and curtain calls, no operatic closing arias, no mind-bending twists … no karmic justice, just ignominy, never-ending dread and onion rings." Or, as one fan told Time: "Everybody was waiting to see who'd get whacked. But in the end, it was Chase who whacked the viewers." ∎

WILL HART—HBO

THEATER

Playbill Parade

German kids explore their ids, Russian lords cross swords,
and legal eagles meet a blonde whose regal in the year onstage

Spring Awakening

Rocker Duncan Sheik's musical
version of Frank Wedekind's
1891 Expressionist play about
German adolescents exploring
their sexuality, above, was a
surprise hit. The ground-
breaking adult musical
garnered eight Tony Awards.

The Coast of Utopia

Tom Stoppard's dissection of
19th century Russia on the
brink of revolution was out-
sized in every way, with a cast
of more than 30 in three full-
length plays. TIME's Richard
Zoglin wondered if that was
"maybe one or two critically
acclaimed plays too many."

TOP: JOAN MARCUS; BOTTOM: PAUL KOLNIK

Legally Blonde: The Musical

When teen girls made a mega-hit of *Wicked,* the 2003 musical version of Gregory Maguire's novel set in the Land of Oz, Broadway producers began seeking other vehicles that would resonate with the pink-and-proud crowd. Enter *Legally Blonde,* based on the 2001 movie hit starring Reese Witherspoon, which tells a girl-power tale of how a campus bubblehead holds her own with the eggheads. Laura Bell Bundy, above, filled Reese's high heels.

Christine Ebersole won unanimous raves for her spectacular dual performances in the musical, playing both the older (in flashbacks) and younger of two eccentric cousins of Jackie O., who were discovered living in squalor in the Hamptons in the 1970s. Ebersole ran away with the Tony Award for Best Leading Actress in a Musical.

Third Time: Charm or Harm?

How many times can Hollywood keep squeezing the same sponge? As many times as moviegoers will shell out their dollars for the tried and true, as the summer of 2007's raft of three-peats proved.

Shrek the Third

Yup, Shrek rhymes with dreck, and a fan of the first two films, TIME critic Richard Corliss, thought this threequel offered too much meandering and moralizing: "Could it be that the buoyancy of pastiche comedy is harder to sustain the third time around?"
Earnings: $790 million *(all earnings are worldwide)*

Pirates of the Caribbean: At World's End

Or should that be "at wit's end"? Johnny Depp was back as Jack Sparrow, role model Keith Richards did a brief cameo as his daddy, and buckles got swashed.
Booty: $958 million

The Bourne Ultimatum

Matt Damon gave fans another thrill ride in the third of the films based on Robert Ludlum's popular tales of amnesia and espionage. Critics and audiences approved.
Earnings: $396 million

Spider-Man 3

Director Sam Raimi and stars Toby Maguire and Kirsten Dunst returned to weave another story of young-adult, superhero blues, spiced up with special effects. It was a hit, even if hero Peter Parker's emo period was lame.
Earnings: $885 million

Earnings: WorldwideBoxOffice.com, through September 2007

Westward, Ho!

Hollywood is back in the saddle again, as a quartet of movie westerns aim to recover some of a lost genre's classic magic

THE HOLLYWOOD WESTERN RODE INTO THE SUNSET long ago, but in 2007 the grand genre resurfaced, struggling to find a foothold in a marketplace teeming with comic-book superheroes, raunchy teen comedies and violent slasher films. In the 1950s the western tale was ubiquitous, both on the big screen (where such stars as Brando, Gable, Monroe and Stanwyck did sagebrush epics) and on TV (where, in the 1958-59 season, six of the seven top-rated series were oaters). A decade later, the form was revitalized in the spaghetti westerns starring Clint Eastwood and directed by Sergio Leone. But by the late 1970s the genre had virtually bit the dust. Natural western stars might very occasionally be able to get on a horse and shoot it out—like Eastwood in *Unforgiven* or Kevin Costner in *Dances with Wolves* and *Open Range*—but only through an expenditure of their clout.

Westerns didn't exactly thunder into town in 2007; they tiptoed in, as if aware that they were made only because some potent actor like Brad Pitt invested his cachet in producing an epic-size movie on an indie-film budget (his starring vehicle, *The Assassination of Jesse James by the Coward Robert Ford*, was produced for a modest $30 million or so). Or because two boutique studios chipped in for a modern western revenge film, as Paramount Vantage and Miramax did for Joel and Ethan Coen's smart, violent and defiantly quirky *No Country for Old Men*. Or because a director with a hit movie on his résumé charmed financiers outside the studio. That's how James Mangold, fresh from *Walk the Line*, got to remake the 1957 western *3:10 to Yuma*, with Russell Crowe and Christian Bale.

"There's an assumption in Hollywood that the western doesn't have a built-in audience," Mangold told TIME. "The adults who might want to go don't go to the movies, and the young ones are locked into the superhero world ... The movie industry is basically built on serving 14-year-old males, and they aren't interested in rural America." Then there's the problem of tempo. Other modern movies move at warp speed, but the cowboy hero is a man with a slow hand. As Christopher Frayling, author of biographies of Eastwood and Leone, notes, "You can speed up spaceships and cars, but you can't speed up horses."

KIMBERLY FRENCH—WARNER BROTHERS

No Country for Old Men
Brothers Joel and Ethan Coen, the creators of such offbeat classics as *Fargo* and *O Brother, Where Art Thou?*, light out for the territories in this typically twisted version of Cormac McCarthy's acclaimed novel. Tommy Lee Jones, Javier Bardem, Josh Brolin, above, and a clutch of other Coen-friendly stars shine in this modern-dress reimagining of the western tale.

Sukiyaki Western: Django
Japan has a long history of creating memorable westerns; Hollywood adapted the "sukiyaki westerns" of Akira Kurosawa to make such classics as *The Magnificent Seven* and *A Fistful of Dollars*. Takashi Miike's wildly imaginative *Sukiyaki Western: Django*, above, played to rapt crowds at the 2007 Venice and Toronto film festivals but did not find a U.S. distributor.

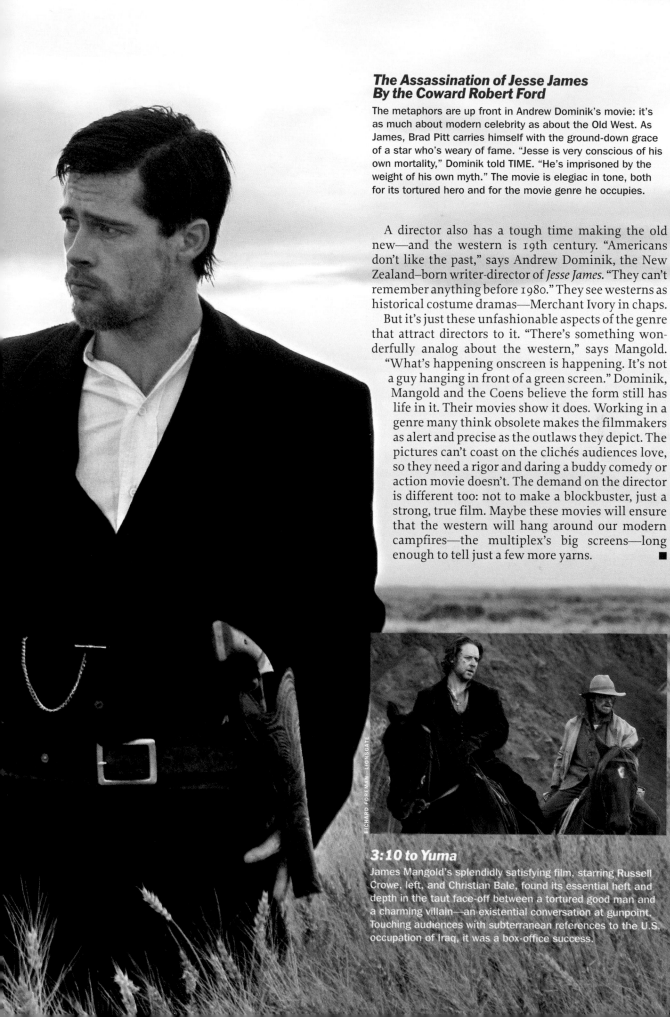

The Assassination of Jesse James
By the Coward Robert Ford

The metaphors are up front in Andrew Dominik's movie: it's as much about modern celebrity as about the Old West. As James, Brad Pitt carries himself with the ground-down grace of a star who's weary of fame. "Jesse is very conscious of his own mortality," Dominik told TIME. "He's imprisoned by the weight of his own myth." The movie is elegiac in tone, both for its tortured hero and for the movie genre he occupies.

A director also has a tough time making the old new—and the western is 19th century. "Americans don't like the past," says Andrew Dominik, the New Zealand–born writer-director of *Jesse James*. "They can't remember anything before 1980." They see westerns as historical costume dramas—Merchant Ivory in chaps. But it's just these unfashionable aspects of the genre that attract directors to it. "There's something wonderfully analog about the western," says Mangold. "What's happening onscreen is happening. It's not a guy hanging in front of a green screen." Dominik, Mangold and the Coens believe the form still has life in it. Their movies show it does. Working in a genre many think obsolete makes the filmmakers as alert and precise as the outlaws they depict. The pictures can't coast on the clichés audiences love, so they need a rigor and daring a buddy comedy or action movie doesn't. The demand on the director is different too: not to make a blockbuster, just a strong, true film. Maybe these movies will ensure that the western will hang around our modern campfires—the multiplex's big screens—long enough to tell just a few more yarns. ∎

3:10 to Yuma

James Mangold's splendidly satisfying film, starring Russell Crowe, left, and Christian Bale, found its essential heft and depth in the taut face-off between a tortured good man and a charming villain—an existential conversation at gunpoint. Touching audiences with subterranean references to the U.S. occupation of Iraq, it was a box-office success.

Notebook

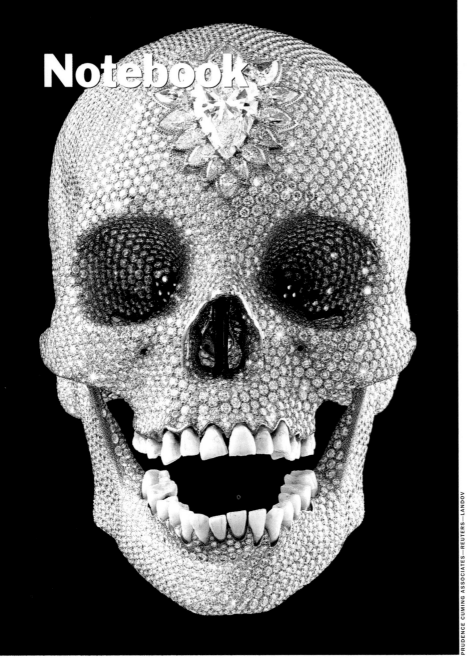

All That Glitters

Death and dollars brought fame to British "shock artist" Damien Hirst, 42, in the '90s: he won renown for works that consisted of sheep and sharks, often cut in two, suspended in tanks of formaldehyde, and he became the world's priciest living artist in 2006, when his *Lullaby Spring* sold for more than $19 million at auction. In 2007 Hirst fused his two passions, encrusting a skull with hundreds of diamonds and calling it *For the Love of God.* It sold for a rumored $100 million. The price is a secret, as is the identity of the group that bought it, save for one tantalizing hint: the partnership is known to include Hirst, who often invests in his own work. Wouldn't you?

Radiohead's Freebie

The loyal fans of rock's most consistently innovative band have been salivating for years at the prospect of a new album, their anticipation jazzed by the 2006 tour debut of 13 new songs that, as usual, alternated between paranoia and romance, feedback and melody. But the British quartet hesitated because, among other reasons, their contract with record company EMI lapsed in 2003. Numerous big-label suitors called at the band's Oxford, England, headquarters, but all were rebuffed. In October, Thom Yorke and his mates shocked a music business still troubled by digital file sharing by releasing their seventh album, *In Rainbows,* as a digital download for which buyers could pay any price they chose, including nothing. The average price paid in the first week on sale: $8.

Offstage Dramas

Late in 2007, a pair of union strikes—the first by film and television writers, the second by Broadway stagehands—put management and workers in the nation's powerful entertainment industry at odds. The writers went on strike first, walking off their jobs on Nov. 5 and setting up picket lines in both Hollywood and New York City. At issue was their demand to receive a bigger slice of the revenues from the use of films and TV shows on both DVDs and the Internet. Writers claim they were burned in the '90s when they agreed to a low fee scale for use of their work on DVDs.

Stagehands struck Broadway theaters on Nov. 10, in a dispute over the number of backstage workers needed to open plays and keep them running; the two sides struck a deal and curtains went up on Nov 29—but the writers remained on strike as of early December.

WARNER BROTHERS (2)

A Surprise Smash

The musclebound epic *300*, a retelling in graphic-novel style of the Spartans' heroic defense at Thermopylae in 480 B.C., earned $456 million globally—a remarkable showing for a film by a young director that starred nobody in particular. It may have been the audience's body love—for pecs so massive and heads so handsome (before decapitation)— because Zack Snyder's movie was otherwise a garrulous history lesson that took itself way too seriously, declared TIME critic Lev Grossman.

So why was the film Hollywood's biggest surprise of 2007? Perhaps because it was a violent, beautiful movie that looked like nothing audiences ever seen. Very little in *300* was real except the actors. Sets, locations, armies, blood—all were computer generated, using the blue-screen technology shown at left. Indeed, *300* may represent the future of filmmaking. Snyder, who cut his teeth on high-concept, effects-heavy TV commercials, is one of a small, hypertechnical fringe of directors who are exploring a new way to make movies by discarding props, sets, extras and real-life locations and replacing them with computer-generated equivalents.

Cinema has always had a tenuous connection to reality; Snyder and his ilk are severing it almost completely. The bottom line: the film's total production cost was $60 million, so it earned almost 8 times its cost. Now that's a special effect.

Feeding the Flame

Canadian indie-rock band Arcade Fire scored a big hit with their second album, *Neon Bible*. It takes some doing to make an album darker than *Funeral*, their 2005 debut, but leader Win Butler is adept at cataloging his gloom. "Every spark of friendship and love/ Will die without a home," he yelps on *Intervention*, one of the happier new tunes. Young rockers often mistake darkness for depth, and Butler may outgrow it. For now, *Neon Bible* has it both ways, getting audiences to sing along with its optimistic-sounding anthems about pessimism.

RYAN REMIORZ—CP—AP IMAGES

Milestones

IRA NOWINSKI—CORBIS

1935-2007

Luciano Pavarotti
Voice of a generation

He became a star in America in 1971 at New York City's Metropolitan Opera, after hitting a stunning nine consecutive high C's in Donizetti's *La Fille du Régiment*, but Luciano Pavarotti had become an opera divo many years earlier. As a 4-year-old child, he suddenly jumped onto the kitchen table of his family's home in Modena, Italy, one day and began belting out *La donna e mobile*. Bravo! The King of the high C's, who had little classical training and could barely read sheet music, went on to become the most popular tenor of all time, selling more than 50 million albums and winning five Grammys.

However large, such numbers can't do justice to a voice that was otherworldly in its beauty, bringing tears to the eyes of opera élitists who had every reason to dislike this unapologetic populist. But Pavarotti, seen here in 1979, also won raves from a tougher crowd: millions of people who had no interest in opera until they heard him sing, like the PBS viewers who watched endless repeats of his *Three Tenors* specials with José Carreras and Placido Domingo, or the soccer fans who fell in love with Puccini's *Nessun dorma* after he performed it at the 1990 World Cup final. At his funeral in Modena, a recording of a young Pavarotti singing a duet with his father—a baker who also wanted to be a tenor—brought the weeping congregation to its feet in a standing ovation. It was his last curtain call. ∎

1912-2007

Lady Bird Johnson
A First Lady who spurred the greening of America

S HE WAS BORN CLAUDIA ALTA TAYLOR, BUT BY THE
time she was 2, her nursemaid had declared
that she was "pretty as a lady bird." And with
that, her name was decided. Her fate was decided in
1934: after she graduated from the University of Texas
at Austin with degrees in history and journalism, she
met an ambitious former teacher named Lyndon
Johnson. They married three months after that, and
she went from studying history to making it.

With her husband, she was catapulted into the
White House by the murder of John F. Kennedy. Her
predecessor as First Lady was Jacqueline Kennedy—
to put it mildly, a hard act to follow. Wisely, she didn't
try to play Jackie; her own style was modest, warm
and comforting—what a traumatized country needed.

But she also had an agenda: she called it beautification. At a time when environmentalism was a word
few had heard, she did more to make Americans aware
of the beauty and fragility of their natural surroundings
than anyone since Teddy Roosevelt. Before there was an
Earth Day, there was Lady Bird, pursuing her campaign
to preserve national parks, fight pollution, plant wild-
flowers and banish billboards from around federal highways. In 1965 Congress passed the $325 million High-
way Beautification Bill; everybody called it the Lady
Bird Bill.

She adored her husband, ignoring L.B.J.'s roguish
side. She helped reassure suspicious fellow Southern-
ers about his pro–civil rights stances and suffered by
his side over Vietnam. But her countrymen will best
remember her for challenging the U.S. to transform
itself into the song's ideal: America the Beautiful. ■

1931-2007

Boris Yeltsin
Russia's flawed agent of reform

RUSSIA'S FIRST FREELY ELECTED LEADER IN 1,000 years was also one of the most perplexing figures in its history: the transformer who promised reform but later opened fire on his own Parliament, the man on whom the U.S. put all its chips even as Moscow handed the country's assets to a new class of kleptocrats, the man of the people who would become a man of the bottle.

Boris Yeltsin combined a folksy, Reaganesque simplicity with a Nixonian sense of political intrigue (and paranoia) plus a tendency toward accidents that recalled Gerald Ford. On one occasion he was too drunk to leave his plane for a planned meeting with Ireland's Prime Minister—even though, I was told, aides slapped him to bring him to consciousness. But he also had flashes of greatness that made the whole world believe Russia could shed its authoritarian shackles. His defining moment was in August 1991. While Soviet leader Mikhail Gorbachev was summering in the Crimea, dark forces opposed to reform tried to stage a coup. Yeltsin's political instincts were still sharp, and he raced to the scene, outside Russia's White House, where he climbed atop a tank and urged defiance. The putsch failed. Gorbachev returned to Moscow, but when he declared his unshaken faith in the Soviet state, Russia was Yeltsin's. By Christmas, the U.S.S.R. was done. An era of change had begun—though Yeltsin proved unable to master the tumultuous forces he unleashed. ∎

Appreciation by Adi Ignatius, TIME deputy managing editor, who was one of the first Western journalists to interview Yeltsin after he came to power in Russia.

Ingmar Bergman
Stories of God and man, through a lens, darkly

EVEN THOSE WHO NEVER SAW A FILM BY INGMAR Bergman have experienced his influence: gifted directors from Woody Allen to Wes Craven were inspired by the work of this "solemn Swede," and subtle tributes to him show up in places as unlikely as *Bill & Ted's Bogus Journey* and *The Colbert Report*. Not bad for a director who made only one film in English (1971's *The Touch*) and refused for his entire career to work in (or for) Hollywood. It may have been for the best: indelible allegories of postwar man adrift without God generally don't set box-office records on their opening weekend.

In the 1950s and '60s, films like *The Seventh Seal*, *Wild Strawberries* and *Persona* jolted a generation of aspiring filmmakers (and critics) into the realization that, as TIME critic Richard Corliss put it, "[film] is what I want to study, devote my life to." (His work also impressed earlier TIME editors: in 1960 Bergman became the first foreign-language filmmaker to grace its cover since Leni Riefenstahl, Hitler's favorite auteur, in 1936.) In short, Bergman, more than any other filmmaker, made movies matter. As Woody Allen told TIME shortly after Bergman's death, "I think his films have eternal relevance, because [they] deal with ... existential themes that will be relevant 1,000 years from now. When many of the things that are successful and trendy today have been long relegated to musty-looking antiques, his stuff will still be great." ∎

1922-2007

Kurt Vonnegut
Exposing folly with a scalpel of irony

LIKE MARK TWAIN, ANOTHER SATIRIST WITH A KNACK for delivering grim insights with a grin, Kurt Vonnegut—who slightly resembled the creator of Huckleberry Finn—used flippant humor to confront distinctly unfunny issues. Recalling the apocalyptic 1945 firebombing of the German city of Dresden, which he witnessed from the ground as a prisoner of war and survived only because he and other POWs were being held in an underground meat locker when the Allied bombers arrived, Vonnegut would later write, "everything was gone but the cellars, where 135,000 Hansels and Gretels had been baked like gingerbread men." It took Vonnegut more than two decades to come to terms with this horror and write about it in his 1969 masterpiece, *Slaughterhouse-Five*. In later years he tackled such themes as the harmful effects of industry on human beings' collective sense of morality, once saying his goal was to "catch people before they become generals and Senators and Presidents" and "poison their minds with humanity."

Too old to be a peer of the 1960s counterculture generation that shared his world view, he was instead adopted by '60s kids as a kind of cranky uncle, wise and eccentric in equal measure. But the rumpled curmudgeon was also haunted by private demons: he struggled for decades with depression. The man who survived Dresden and a 1984 suicide attempt died from head injuries sustained in a fall. "So it goes." ∎

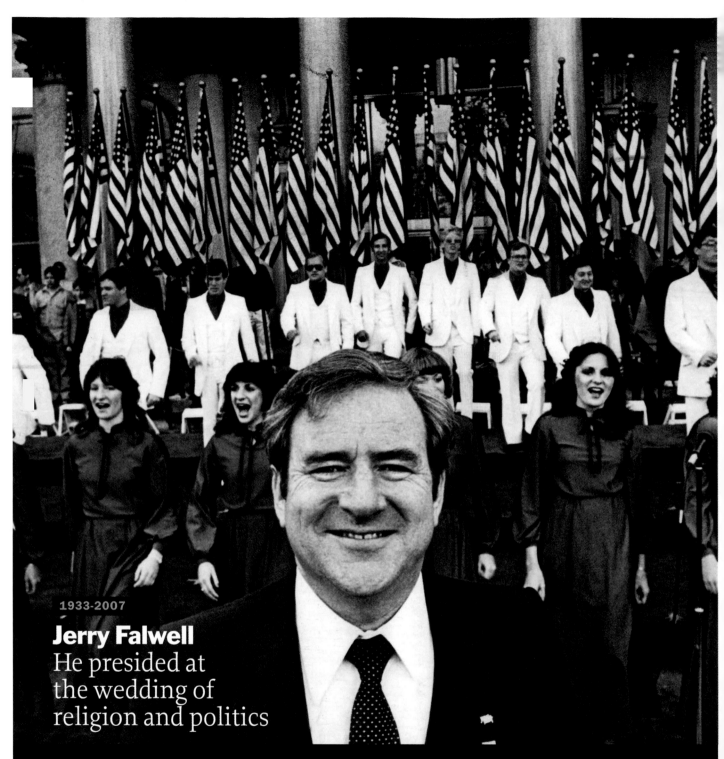

1933-2007

Jerry Falwell
He presided at the wedding of religion and politics

THE SON OF AN AGNOSTIC BOOTLEGGER WHO KILLED his own brother in a gunfight, Jerry Falwell found Jesus at age 18 but didn't find politics until much later—even saying at one point, early in his evangelical career, that "preachers are not called to be politicians but to be soul-winners." Falwell's great American invention was not simply the marriage of religion and politics, since they hadn't lived apart in the first place, but that he united those with religious differences in pursuit of a common political goal. Falwell didn't care that Jimmy Carter was a Bible-believing Baptist if he still had the soul of a Democrat or that Ronald Reagan was a divorced movie star, as long as he was a kindred political spirit.

At a time when you couldn't always get Baptists of different stripes to work together on a bake sale, Falwell founded the Moral Majority in 1979 to be "pro-life, pro-family, pro-morality and pro-American," arguing that Fundamentalist Christians, Orthodox Jews, conservative Roman Catholics and Mormons had so much in common politically that they should overlook their theological divides and concentrate on the political ties that bound them. Helping to register millions of conservative voters, Falwell and his allies substantially aided the landmark election of Reagan the following year and ushered in a decades-long ascendancy of power and influence for the evangelical right that endures to this day. ■

1929-2007

Beverly Sills
The beloved first lady of American opera gave us trills, thrills and chills

BEFORE BROOKLYN-BORN BUBBLES SILVERMAN BE-
came the most popular opera singer of her era,
aspiring divas tended to hail from Europe, where
they were expected to train, then seek the attention of
the major opera houses. Taking the stage name Beverly
Sills, the redheaded child radio star—whose mother
dreamed she'd be the "Jewish Shirley Temple"—stayed
home, loyally working her way up through New York
City's "second" City Opera and drawing raves as a
brilliant coloratura soprano who specialized in splen-
did bel canto roles. Though she appeared around the
globe, the Metropolitan Opera's snooty Rudolf Bing,
who scoffed at U.S.-trained artists, refused her a major
role. Sills' belated 1975 Met premiere, following Bing's
retirement, earned her a 20-minute standing ovation.

Her rise seemed inevitable. Witty, smart, tough
and down-to-earth (she was sometimes called "the
diva next door"), the ebullient performer became a
fine-arts ambassador who was a guest host of the
Tonight Show and sang with the Muppets. She became
a prodigious fund raiser, for special-needs kids (her
son is autistic, her daughter deaf) and for the City
Opera and Lincoln Center, both of which she led after
she retired from singing. Unpretentious offstage as
well as on, she insisted upon democratizing opera by
staging contemporary productions and introducing
supertitles. As beloved as Luciano Pavarotti, she helped
bring opera off its pedestal—and into our hearts. ■

1923-2007

Norman Mailer
The writer
in the arena

HE WAS JUST 25 WHEN HE BECAME ABRUPTLY AND UN-manageably famous. It was 1948, America was looking for its Great War Novel, and there was Norman Mailer, with his jug-handle ears, curly hair, brash voice and *The Naked and the Dead.* The first of his 10 novels and more than two dozen other titles, it became a huge best seller. But fame soon turned fickle on him, or maybe vice versa. Mailer was too flighty, impious and vainglorious to fill the role of anointed American writer as the 1950s conceived it, so for a while his reputation dimmed. But in the decade that followed, he hit his powerful stride with a new kind of metaphysical journalism, as in *The Armies of the*

Night, his brilliant "nonfiction novel" about the October 1967 antiwar march on the Pentagon.

These were the years of Mailer at his most pyro-technic, when he took up every kind of public intellectual battle and even ran a boisterous, quixotic and very entertaining campaign for mayor of New York City. *The Executioner's Song,* the spare and haunting book that came out of the execution of convicted killer Gary Gilmore, is a modern classic. There were many other titles after that, most with moments of genius but none with the same sustained power. Nonetheless, an indispensable, forceful and original cultural voice was lost when Mailer died at 84. ∎

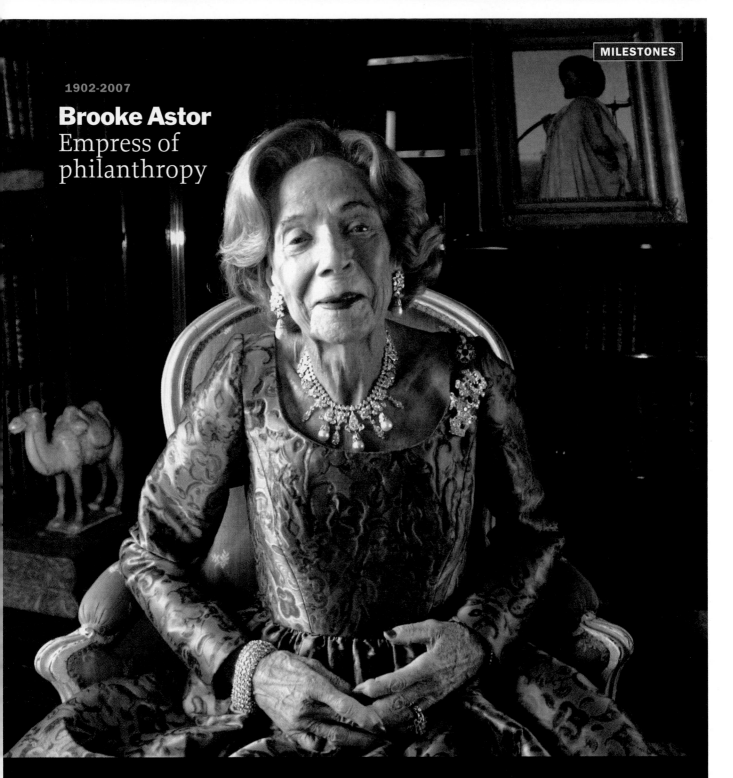

1902-2007

Brooke Astor
Empress of philanthropy

YOU'LL HAVE FUN, POOKIE," A DYING VINCENT ASTOR promised his wife Brooke in 1959, just before he left her $60 million for herself and control of as much again in a foundation dedicated to "the alleviation of human suffering." The merry widow spent her next five decades proving him right. At a time when "high society" seems to consist of heirs run amuck, Brooke Astor harked back to the era of girls gone Wilde: she was a fabulously wealthy woman who was committed to public service and determined to render it with stylish elegance.

Ms. Astor's calling cards were good manners, gentle words and kind deeds. Her mission was to support a stunning list of causes and institutions that served the New York City she deeply loved. Among the recipients of nearly $200 million in Astor largesse distributed before the foundation gave away its last nickel in 1997 were big fish like the Metropolitan Museum of Art, the Bronx Zoo, the New York Public Library, Harlem's Apollo Theater and a host of smaller fry: a boiler for a youth center, a church pipe organ, furniture for homeless families moving into new apartments. "Money is like manure," she liked to say, "It's worthless unless you spread it around." She died at 105, nine years after a grateful New York City named her "a living landmark." ∎

1934-2007

David Halberstam

The legendary journalist won his stripes on tough battlefields, covering the violent days of the civil rights movement in the South, then wading through the streams of Vietnam to unearth the real story of the war, disproving the official line that the U.S. was winning the conflict. He went on to write magisterial volumes that explored American culture through its sports stars, its "best and brightest" Washington players, its media moguls and the lives of the firefighters of a New York City firehouse in the wake of 9/11. The veteran

1932-2007

Liz Claiborne

In 1976, after noting few clothes were made for career moms like herself, the Belgian-born designer started Liz Claiborne Inc. In the 1970s and '80s, her work outfits and sportswear were a revolution—easy, affordable, versatile, sleek. Asked how she became the first woman to found a FORTUNE 500 company, she said, "I listened to the customer."

1925-2007

Art Buchwald

"Dying is easy," Art Buchwald said near the end of his life. "Parking is hard." The satirist's insights won him legions of fans, comparisons to Mark Twain and a Pulitzer Prize. He first generated buzz in the 1950s as a Paris nightlife columnist, then soared to fame in the '60s, skewering the powerful in some 30 books and a column that ran in more than 500 papers. Veteran Washington *Post* editor Ben Bradlee told TIME, "So we outlived Art Buchwald! Big deal! His reputation for gentle, self-deprecating humor will live on ... He made millions of people smile every day. Few of us get to make that kind of contribution to peace and happiness."

1923-2007

Wally Schirra Jr.

The original Mercury 7 astronaut was perfect for the role of brash space pioneer. The only aviator to fly in all three of NASA's first space programs, the garrulous charmer had a blast, smuggling a corned-beef sandwich aboard a Mercury capsule, joking about his pre-launch jitters ("This was all put together by the lowest bidder") and amusing TV viewers with his onboard antics. Yet the cool perfectionist was the go-to guy for such delicate assignments as Gemini 6A—in which he made a critical snap call to stay aboard after an early malfunction on the first launch attempt, and went on to artfully orchestrate the first-ever space rendezvous.

YALE JOEL—TIME LIFE PICTURES

1925-2007

Merv Griffin

If Johnny Carson was TV's aloof arbiter of taste, Merv Griffin was the welcoming show-biz uncle who wanted everyone on his talk show to become a star—including Richard Pryor and George Carlin, whose careers he helped launch. He laughed at his guests' jokes, gushed at their stories and joined them in song, perfecting an easygoing manner that withstood the winds of change. The former Big Band singer was also a creative entrepreneur: in 1964 he came up with *Jeopardy!* (A jack of all trades, he wrote theme music for the show as well.) A decade later, he invented TV's most successful game show, *Wheel of Fortune.* Some called his shows fluff, but the titan of trivia knew his audience: he took the high road, preferring to amuse and inform rather than to titillate.

1920-2007

Leona Helmsley

True, the legendary New York City hotelier was prone to irrational rages in which she summarily dismissed diffident maids or waiters. True, she opined that "only little people pay taxes" and was known as "the Queen of Mean." True, she disinherited two of her grandchildren and left $12 million to her dog, Trouble. But as Helmsley chose to see it, she was just a perfectionist. By all accounts, she adored and was devoted to her real-estate tycoon husband Harry, who was said to have always been spared her wrath. A final truth: in 1989, the testimony of her abused underlings helped convict her for tax evasion, and she spent 19 months in jail.

FRED R. CONRAD—THE NEW YORK TIMES—REDUX

1932-2007

Bowie Kuhn

Take your pick: Bowie Kuhn was either a tone-deaf exec or a valiant guardian of the integrity of the national pastime. The commissioner of Major League Baseball from 1969 to 1984 tangled with stars like Hank Aaron and Jim Bouton and owners like George Steinbrenner, and fought a bitter, losing battle to keep players from free agency. But it was also Kuhn who launched the league playoffs, ruled to open the locker-room door to female writers, inked a deal with NBC to air World Series night games—and saw baseball's attendance triple. Even so, in 1983, team owners angered by his campaign to expose drug use in the game voted to oust him.

AP IMAGES

Ivins

Warren Avis, 89, founded in 1946 the car-rental company that bears his name with two employees, two locations (Miami and Ypsilanti, Mich.) and fewer than 200 cars. He built an empire on the words "We try harder."

Joey Bishop, 89, had the last laugh over his pals in the fabled Las Vegas Rat Pack of the 1960s; the comedian outlived his more celebrated, if less witty, counterparts. In addition to his stand-up duties, Bishop appeared in his own sitcom and filled in as host of the *Tonight Show* some 200 times.

Admiral William Crowe Jr., 82, described by the New York *Times* as "the most powerful peacetime military officer in American history," was appointed Chairman of the Joint Chiefs of Staff by President Ronald Reagan in 1985. The nonconformist Vietnam vet openly condemned the military's "Don't ask, don't tell" policy as anti-gay, sharply criticized the buildup to the first Gulf War and served as U.S. ambassador to Britain during the Clinton Administration.

Michael Deaver, 69, the man TIME called the "vicar of visuals," was Ronald Reagan's media czar. He changed U.S. politics by expertly managing his client's public image with masterly photo ops that played to Reagan's star power.

Thomas Eagleton, 77, was a wry,

straightforward Missouri Democrat whose 18-day stint as the vice-presidential candidate on George McGovern's ticket ended with reports that he had been hospitalized several times for depression.

Steve Fossett, 63, turned to adventuring after making millions in financial services, first swimming the English Channel in 1985. He went on to amass 115 records in the next 22 years in aviation, gliding, ballooning, sailing, boating, mountaineering, skiing, triathlon and dogsledding. On Sept. 3, Fossett did not return from a flight over the Nevada desert in a small plane, as he looked for sites for a projected attempt to break the land-speed record; at press time, his body had not been found.

Robert Goulet, 73, was as handsome as the plastic groom on a wedding cake and also had a sturdy baritone voice; together, they brought him 60 years of fame, beginning with his portrayal of Lancelot in *Camelot* on Broadway in 1960 and continuing through countless TV shows, nightclub shows and cameo appearances.

Don Ho, 76, will be remembered for his laid-back baritone and signature hit, *Tiny Bubbles*, and for personifying the breezy charm of his native Hawaii.

E. Howard Hunt, 88, engineered

Marceau

the Watergate break-in as an aide to Richard Nixon. The former CIA operative (and author of more than 80 spy novels) served 33 months in prison for his role in the scandal.

Molly Ivins, 62, whose columns skewered the high and mighty, famously referred to George W. Bush as "Shrub." She could write with heartfelt earnestness yet just

Roach

as naturally characterize height-challenged politicians as "runts with attitudes."

Richard Jewell, 44, was initially hailed as a hero, after he helped evacuate an area after a bomb blast at the 1996 Olympic Games in Atlanta. Then he was reviled as a villain when the FBI leaked his name as its primary suspect; finally, he was seen as a victim after investigators exonerated Jewell later that year. (In 2005, Eric Rudolph confessed to the attack.)

Deborah Kerr, 86, was too tall to pursue her first love, ballet, so she turned to the screen, making her mark in roles in *The King and I, An Affair to Remember* and *From Here to Eternity,* in which she shared a famously sandy kiss with co-star Burt Lancaster.

Teddy Kollek, 95, Jerusalem's breezy, liberal, secular mayor for 28 years, delicately balanced the needs of its fractious citizens and helped transform the battered city into one of the most culturally vibrant in the Middle East.

Marcel Marceau, 84, spoke five languages including his native French, but the public seldom heard him utter a word: the world's most famous mime was responsible for reviving the art form.

Tammy Faye Messner, 65, was a 1980s caricature—the garish, bejeweled wife of wealthy televangelist Jim Bakker and the co-host of *The Jim and Tammy Show.*

Max Roach, 83, helped found the revolutionary genre of bebop and made percussion a star player. He backed Duke Ellington and Charlie Parker as a teenager and created rich, complex percussive sounds.

Mstislav Rostropovich, 80, was an ebullient, incendiary cellist-maestro who became a global star, both for his magically rich, airy tones and his political courage in standing up to the rulers of the Soviet Union.

Arthur Schlesinger Jr., 86, was a liberal in the decades when liberalism was in fashion, and he remained an "unreconstructed and unrepentant" man of the left long after the left had lost its steam. The brilliant Harvard historian made the awkward leap to public service when John F. Kennedy brought him to the White House as a policy

Snyder

Rostropovich

adviser. His more than 20 books included two Pulitzer-prizewinning works, *The Age of Jackson* (1945) and the 1966 best seller on J.F.K.'s presidency, *A Thousand Days.* He helped change the way Americans thought about their nation, arguing eloquently for "ideas, vision and courage … things seldom produced by committees."

Anna Nicole Smith, 39, the signature blond bombshell of her era, died from a lethal mix of prescription drugs after collapsing in her hotel room in Hollywood, Fla.

Ian Smith, 88, was Rhodesia's last white Prime Minister, and until his death he stoutly defended his white-minority government's 14-year reign over the nation's 5 million blacks. The right-winger declared independence from Britain in 1965 and survived raging civil wars, sanctions and global disdain until 1980, when he stepped down and Rhodesia became Zimbabwe.

Tom Snyder, 71, made a huge hit of his late-night *Tomorrow* show in the 1970s. Utterly authentic and at ease, the veteran journalist laid the groundwork for future late-night stars like David Letterman.

Frank Stanton, 98, turned a string of radio stations into the CBS Television Network; went on to make stars of such figures as Edward R. Murrow, Walter Cronkite and Jackie Gleason; and trumped rival NBC by securing the acquisition of a promising new sitcom, *I Love Lucy.*

Paul Tibbets Jr., 92, climbed into his B-29 aircraft, the *Enola Gay*—named after his mother—on Aug. 6, 1945, and dropped the first atom bomb over the city of Hiroshima, Japan. Nearly 80,000 people lost their lives on that single day, but Tibbets never expressed remorse. "I sleep clearly every night," he once said. Like President Harry Truman, who ordered the bombing, Tibbets believed that the deed forced an early end to World War II in the Pacific, thus preventing an Allied invasion of Japan's chain of home islands that might have resulted in the deaths of millions of Americans and Japanese. Fearful of protesters, Tibbets requested that no funeral arrangements be made and no headstone mark his grave site.

Schlesinger

Jack Valenti, 85, ran the Motion Picture Association of America for four successful decades. Hollywood's lobbyist-ambassador was also one of Lyndon Johnson's closest White House aides during the advent of the Great Society and the turmoil of the mid-1960s.

Porter Wagoner, 80, was the king of country glam. The Grand Ole Opry legend's blond pompadour, rhinestone suits and strong voice made him a hitmaker (*Green Green Grass of Home, Satisfied Mind*), but he was best known for mentoring and performing with Dolly Parton early in her career.